Holding Avery

Holding Avery

A Memoir

Heidi Chandler

MP PUBLISHING

Holding Avery

First edition published in 2014 by

MP Publishing
12 Strathallan Crescent, Douglas, Isle of Man IM2 4NR British Isles
mppublishingusa.com

Jacket designed by Alison Graihagh Crellin.

Publisher's Cataloging-in-Publication data
Chandler, Heidi.
    Holding Avery : a memoir / Heidi Chandler.
    p. cm.
    ISBN 978-1-84982-304-3

1. Chandler, Heidi. 2. Miscarriage --Patients --Biography. 3. Pregnant women --United States --Biography. 4. Perinatal death --Psychological aspects. 5. Fetal death --Psychological aspects. 6. Bereavement. I. Title.

618.3/92 --dc23
RG648 .C43 2014

ISBN 978-1-84982-304-3
10 9 8 7 6 5 4 3 2 1
Also available in eBook

For Avery.

"Perhaps they are not the stars, but rather openings in Heaven where the love of our lost ones pours through and shines down upon us to let us know they are happy."

~Author Unknown

CHAPTER ONE

Four years ago my daughter died. She wasn't murdered by a psychopath on her way home from school or struck by a drunk driver while riding her hot pink Big Wheel through our clean, safe suburban streets. I didn't watch her grow pale and weak and slowly waste away from cancer or another equally terrible disease. My daughter died a very quiet death, an unexpected death, a death that leaves parents wandering in a haze of confusion and everyone else dumb with silence. When I speak of her, it tends to be a painful, awkward conversation. People shift uncomfortably, avert their eyes, find a way to change the subject. I really can't blame them. For my daughter is a sad reminder that not all pregnancies end in smiles and kisses and dirty diapers and sleepless nights.

You see, my daughter died before she was ever born.

If you listen to some people, and in many states, legally, that means my daughter never lived. I suppose that's true, in a way. I never got to see her open her big brown eyes. I never watched her learn to crawl. I never heard her giggle or felt the weight of her warm, vibrant body as I rocked her to sleep singing off-key lullabies written just for her. I never saw my girl run and jump and laugh and play and sing and dance and smile and grow and live.

After she died, people said, "At least you didn't really know her. At least you didn't watch her grow up and then lose her. That would be horrible."

Perhaps my way was better. But it still hurt like hell.

CHAPTER TWO

There are very few truly defining moments in life, and it took me three decades to have my first. Up until my daughter's death I coasted through my days, believing the mundane was important and the important life or death. I had a good life, a happy life, what some might call an easy life.

The daughter of two small-town northern Michigan doctors, I was blessed with a cheerful, carefree childhood spent frolicking in the woods of our modern-day Mayberry. Summers were endless days of climbing tall oaks, catching frogs, and cannonballing into the crisp, spring-fed waters of Heart Lake. My biggest worries were how long I could stand on a floating inner tube and whether I could keep my marshmallow from burning in the campfire.

Winters were cold and snowy and dark by four p.m., but that didn't keep us from skiing, sledding, and building magical child-sized castles out of the snow and ice. We made our own anatomically correct Frosty the Snowmen and littered the yard in snow angels. After hours playing in the tundra, our frozen fingers were thawed with homemade chicken soup and hot chocolate next to a crackling fire.

In many ways I was the all-American girl-next-door—cute, blonde, bubbly, and full of life. I baked cookies, played the piano, got A's in school, and could throw a mean spiral. But behind that veil of wholesome Americana was a stereotypical teenager, egotistical and insecure, obsessed with being the coolest, the smartest, the prettiest, and the best at everything. I could be

sweet and demure one second and a devious bitch the next—
but no matter how much trouble I caused, I always knew I had
a family who loved me.

I left the comfort of my small town and started college at
Michigan State University as an immature seventeen-year-old,
where I quickly realized that I wasn't the coolest, the smartest, or
the prettiest. It was a shock, but slowly I learned the world didn't
revolve around me and I really wasn't that special after all. But
I was still blessed with a good head on my shoulders and didn't
have to study hard to do well, which allowed me to have more
than my share of fun.

Weekends were a blur of tailgates, keg parties, and trying
to catch the eye of the cutest guy in the room. I fell in love. I
had my heart broken. I broke a few hearts. I learned to do keg
stands and tequila shots and how to get a fake ID. I also learned
how to be humble and open-minded. And somewhere in there
I got a halfway decent education, too.

I graduated with a journalism degree and reluctantly joined
the real world. I was courteous and intelligent, so finding
jobs turned out to be easy for me. I had jobs I loved, jobs I
hated, people I loved, people I hated. Each step in my life
was instrumental in making me who I am, yet it all blends
together into a murky concoction of happy and sad, terrible
and wonderful. No one moment is clearly defined.

I knew I'd eventually have kids. I thought I'd have a boy and
a girl, like my parents, but I wasn't one of those girls with baby
names picked out decades in advance. I lived my life in the
present and figured I'd think about kids when it was time to
have them.

When Chris and I married in 2004 at the ages of twenty-
six and twenty-seven, after a six-year courtship, we weren't
ready for parenthood. We were too busy having fun, earning
our reputation as the quintessential party couple. Not the hard-
partying, snorting-cocaine-with-movie-stars-in-the-bathroom
kind of party couple, but the relatively tame football-and-
barbecue type. We were the people you could count on to throw

the parties, and, if the festivities took place at your house, we were the first to arrive and the last to leave.

Chris and I met my last year of college, fell in love with each other's youthful exuberance, and opted to continue our carefree lifestyle well into adulthood. We were responsible people with good jobs—me as a high school journalism teacher, Chris as a purchasing guru—but we were our own Mich Ultra commercial. We worked hard and played hard. We did everything within our power to hold onto our youth, to seize every last ounce of foolish pleasure we could, because we knew it would inevitably come to an end. We looked at the "adults" around us—they were so tired, so boring, so defeated. Starting a family meant we would officially be adults, and we weren't in any hurry to join that club.

When I hit thirty I began receiving unsolicited comments from the peanut gallery. Family dinners were met with a barrage of "Are you guys thinking about kids?" Nearly every phone conversation with my mother featured references to my eggs drying up. Our friends were dropping babies left and right; whenever we saw them, proudly toting their pink, squirming offspring, they became serious and whispered, "Are you guys trying?"

I was disturbed how concerned the world was with our sex life.

I'm a fairly private person, and I found the inquisition into my uterus terribly annoying. The more people bothered me about having kids, the less I wanted them. My uterus was my own business, thank you very much, and if my womb was barren or my husband was shooting blanks I certainly wasn't about to share it with the rest of the world. Didn't people realize how rude they were? Yet the questions persisted, so I started having fun with it. At Thanksgiving dinner, the jaws of my husband's Italian Catholic family dropped in one simultaneous thud when I responded to the requisite kid question with, "I'm not particularly fond of little people."

A few weeks later another relative cornered me, asking if we would be having kids soon. "Nope." I smiled, walking away.

When I turned thirty-one something in me changed. Chris and I loved being together, but as time marched on, we grew bored with each other. It was a boredom that lingered, one that couldn't be squelched by vacations to Cabo or romantic nights out. We still enjoyed our life together, but something was missing. After much internal deliberation, I realized that missing piece was a child. I decided that after one last summer of carefree fun, we'd start trying to get pregnant. (I didn't tell Chris of my decision until the fall; I didn't want to be locked in.)

I clearly remember the Sunday night in late September when I told Chris I was ready to start trying for a baby. We were in bed, curled up in the dark discussing our day, one of my favorite things to do. It was a warm night, one of the last before the cold, rainy Michigan fall set in. The windows were open; crickets and other mysterious creatures of the night offered a soothing soundtrack to our low voices. I'd been trying for a good ten minutes to casually work my announcement into the conversation, but the words were stuck in my mouth like a sleeve of saltines. Once I said it there was no turning back; it would completely change our lives. I didn't know if I was ready for that.

Chris finally said goodnight and rolled over. I lay there, eyes wide, listening to his breathing. It became slower and heavier.

"Honey?" I whispered, hoping he was asleep.

"Hmmm?" he replied groggily.

"I think we should have a baby," I mumbled, chills running the length of my body.

He sat straight up in bed, instantly awake. "What?" he asked, his voice pitched up with excitement. "Did you say what I think you just said?"

"Well, yeah. If we're going to do it this year, we need to start trying now," I muttered, going into a short justification. Considering my job as a teacher, we had what was called the "teacher window" (the window of opportunity to conceive so that the baby is born in early summer, thus not interfering with work). I loved my career, and I didn't want to worry about taking maternity leave.

My husband stared me down in the darkness, trying to read my body language. I could tell he had been waiting for this moment. "Are you sure?" he asked.

"Yes," I whispered.

"Positive?"

"Yes."

"Then let's do it."

Thus began our first try, though I'll spare you the details.

I wish I could say I was overcome with joy at the thought of becoming pregnant, but that wasn't the case. Long after my husband had fallen asleep I lay awake, questioning my decision. It was very possible that at that very moment a life was coming into being inside me, and it made me sick. I was shaking a little, and sweating. Did I really want a baby? Would I be a good mother? How do you know what to do with a baby? I was going to get fat. I couldn't drink. My in-laws were never going to leave us alone. Was I too selfish to have a child? Endless thoughts swirled in my head like winter snow for hours, finally drifting to a halt around three a.m. when, terrified and exhausted, I fell asleep.

Weeks went by and we continued to try, not in the overzealous way that involves fertility calculators and ovulation kits, but just casual sex here and there. We lived under the motto, "Whatever happens, happens." I was still scared about the possibility of becoming a mother, but I was never one to be an open book, so I kept my reservations to myself.

When my period came in the middle of October, I actually breathed a big sigh of relief. In the next second I became depressed that I wasn't pregnant. I was a walking contradiction; I couldn't even decide what I wanted.

In truth, I wasn't good at making monumental decisions. I spent the majority of my life letting other people make my important choices for me. I listened to my parents, my friends, my husband...it was easier that way, and I never really had to listen to myself. Now here I was, facing one of the biggest decisions of my life, and I was terrified because it was all up to me.

In the midst of my sea of uncertainty, there was one thing I did know. My window was quickly coming to a close, and I was looking at waiting another year to have a baby. I was sad, but also relieved. I had tried, hadn't I? And it hadn't happened. The higher powers had spoken; it wasn't time for me to be a mother. I could deal with that—I could wait another year. As October came to a close, I officially decided to throw in the towel, and Chris was once again relegated to wearing the dreaded condom.

My husband, however, a born salesman, wasn't quite finished. The Wednesday before Halloween, after dinner and a few cocktails at our local watering hole, he talked me into one last try. What could it hurt, I thought. If I hadn't gotten knocked up yet, it certainly wasn't going to happen this one time. So we had one last unprotected hurrah before the window was officially closed and locked.

I remember in Technicolor the day I took that first pregnancy test. I have what I like to call an overactive period; it comes every twenty-three days, and it always comes. It has since I was eleven years old, completely traumatized by the mess in my pants at Sixth Grade Camp. So when day twenty-four came and went, I freaked out. I spent my entire workday running to the bathroom every fifteen minutes "just to check," and when the school day ended I decided to stop by the pharmacy. I knew that pregnancy tests weren't completely accurate that early, but I needed to take one for my own sanity. Just to be safe, I bought the bulk pack.

I wiped a stray bead of sweat from my forehead and placed the box on the counter to check out. My face was flushed, my hands shaking.

The clerk, a plump, graying woman in her fifties, stared at me with a quizzical smile. "Is this a good thing, honey?" she asked.

"Huh?" I replied anxiously. I felt naughty, like I'd just been caught in the middle of a crack deal.

"The test." She pointed at the counter. "Is it a good thing or a bad thing you have to take it?"

"Oh. Yeah. A good thing, I think," I answered, forcing a smile. "I think it's a good thing."

I went home and sat on the couch, my heart racing. Should I call Chris? Should I wait for him to come home so we could do it together? I hadn't shared my suspicions. I tied my long blond hair into a ponytail like I was about to work out, took a deep breath, and decided to just take the test; I was a big girl, and I was determined to do it on my own. I forced myself into the bathroom and peed on the stick, struggling to keep my hands steady. My head danced and I felt the urge to vomit as I waited five agonizing minutes, unsure if my nausea was from anxiety or the tiny seed rooting in my uterus. If it was positive, I would have been pregnant long before the test confirmed it, yet the ignorance of not knowing was beautiful. Once I really knew, my life would instantly change. I hated change. I could hear my heart beating in the silence of the bathroom.

I checked the clock. Time was up. Just to be safe, I waited one more minute, counting the numbers aloud. Finally, I took a deep breath and mustered the courage to pick up the little plastic stick that told my future. I stared at it hard. There were two pink lines. Maybe. There was definitely one line, but the second was faint. I reread the directions; even a faint line could mean I was pregnant. "Could" mean I was pregnant? I wanted a definitive yes or no, not a "could." I started getting angry. Why hadn't I splurged on the more expensive test, the one for idiots, the one that gives dummies like me a simple "pregnant" or "not pregnant"? No—the most important moment of my life, and I had been ruled by economics.

Or maybe I just hadn't followed the directions. I unfolded the paper insert and slowly read them over again, this time out loud, making sure I'd followed each step correctly. I was frustrated and on the verge of tears. Peeing on a stick wasn't supposed to be so difficult. Yet here I was, with two college degrees, and I couldn't even figure out a Goddamn pregnancy test. And I was supposed to take care of a baby?

This kid didn't stand a chance.

Angrily, I pulled out another test and returned to the toilet, squeezing out all of the pee I could. My bladder was empty, so I drank more water and took one more test.

Each stick looked the same: six pink lines staring at me from the bathroom counter, taunting me with reality.

I had to call Chris. Shaking, I dialed him at work.

"What's wrong?" he asked.

"Nothing," I said, unable to recognize my own voice.

"Okay...." He didn't believe me.

I didn't know what to say. I panicked. I was doing it all wrong, calling him at work. I should wrap the test in a cute little bow and leave it on his nightstand for him to find when he came home. I should leap into his outstretched arms with excitement while we smothered each other with kisses in anticipation of the new life that had been created by our undying love. That's what a good wife was supposed to do. I should be ecstatic with the anticipation of the upcoming nine months. I was supposed to rub my belly excitedly, coo about baby names, and pee myself over tiny pink and blue booties.

"I'm pregnant," I blurted out.

Silence.

Oh great, I thought. Now he's going to leave me for his secretary.

"Hello?" I asked.

"Yeah, I'm here. You just took me by surprise. Good."

"Good?"

"Yeah, good."

I was glad he was taking it well. I, on the other hand, was on the verge of a meltdown.

"Listen, I have to go," he said. "We'll talk more about this when I get home, okay?"

"Okay," I whispered meekly, returning the phone to its cradle.

So that was it. I was pregnant and my husband knew. Now what? I couldn't just go sit on the couch and watch TV. I needed to get online and do research. I needed to go buy baby clothes and cribs and blankets and diapers and the whole world for this baby. There was so much to do, and I only had nine months to prepare.

While I was cleaning up the bathroom I caught a glimpse of my reflection in the mirror. Did I look different? I lifted up my sweater and stared at my relatively flat tummy, amazed that at that very moment a human being was busy growing inside, a mess of cells and tissue and DNA that would eventually turn into my child. It was remarkable, terrifying, and impossible for my brain to process.

I went and sat on the couch and watched Oprah, attempting to numb myself with daytime television. It didn't work.

For the next few days, I didn't know what to do. I wasn't ready to make an appointment to see a doctor, since I had no idea what doctor I wanted to go to. Plus it was very early in my pregnancy, and I remembered reading that a large percentage of pregnancies end in miscarriage in the first couple of weeks. I didn't want to get too attached. So I investigated doctors, bought prenatal vitamins, and went about my life.

Two weeks passed and life continued to be completely normal. I had no morning sickness, no nausea. I wasn't tired, and I felt good enough to run three miles every day. I was starving all the time, but that wasn't anything new for me. By the time I finally went to the doctor I was actually skeptical about my pregnancy. Maybe something was wrong with my girl parts?

The waiting room was filled with women. The twenty-something to my right was glowing, cradling her tiny baby bump, while I feared the enormous lady seated across from us was either going to eat me or squat and give birth to her child right there in the waiting room. Chris held my hand and smiled.

"Please tell me I'm not going to get that huge," I whispered. He squeezed my hand and laughed.

We were ushered into a small office where we met with a nurse, filled out paperwork, and were given the lay of the land concerning the three doctors who worked in the practice. I would rotate through each doctor during the course of my pregnancy. Since we didn't know which doctor would be on call when I went into labor, they wanted to ensure I was comfortable with all of them.

Finally, after an hour of administrative jargon, we met with an actual doctor. According to the "magic wheel of conception," I was about six weeks along; too early to really do anything or see anything, he said. So I had a quick pelvic exam, set up an appointment in four weeks, and went off to the lab to have blood drawn.

And that was it. I went home completely unfulfilled and still not feeling pregnant.

Time continued to pass quickly, and I shuffled through my days in a fog, waiting for something big to happen to make my pregnancy authentic. We hadn't told anyone, so it was still our little secret, and it was eating away at me.

The fact that I had an actual person growing inside me was entirely surreal.

How could my life be changing but be exactly the same? How could my body be creating a life but still look and feel the same? I needed a sign that there was actually a baby in my belly. Until I got one, I was living in a dream.

The next time we went to the doctor, I finally got that sign.

I saw the same doctor I had seen at my initial visit. He was cordial, asked a few questions about how I was feeling, told me how lucky I was to have avoided morning sickness, and then proceeded to the moment I'd been waiting for since I first stared at that little pee-covered stick.

I lay down on the exam table and lifted up my sweater. (I still remember exactly what I was wearing, a tan sweater with brown plaid dress pants from The Limited. I was so proud those pants still fit me.) The doctor slathered my still-flat belly with warm jelly and reached for the hand-held Doppler. Slowly, carefully, he rubbed the magical machine back and forth across my stomach. I was instantly treated to the soothing whooshing sounds of my own uterus, but no heartbeat.

I knew it, I thought, taking a deep breath. This pregnancy is a hoax.

I gazed up at Chris, who was studying my belly with a furrowed brow. We both looked to the doctor, awaiting an explanation.

He was serious, a man focused on his work. As we watched him, the corner of his narrow lips curled into a small smile as the device picked up the sweet sound of a tiny, fast-beating heart.

Clop-clop. Clop-clop.

I pictured wild horses running through the prairie.

"That's the heartbeat," the doctor said, smiling. "It's a good, strong heartbeat."

I am not a crier, but I couldn't stop the tears from puddling in my eyes. Don't do it, I whispered in my head. Not here. Do not cry.

It's very cliché, but in that instant I was overcome with love, a kind of love I had never experienced before—the kind of love only a mother can comprehend. It was truly overwhelming, the spectrum of feelings I instantly developed for the tiny little heart in my belly, the tiny little human being that had decided to take up residence inside of me. In a nanosecond, I had fallen deeply in love with a person I had never met before, and it was simply beautiful. Even though I didn't know this child, I instantly knew that I would go to the ends of the earth to protect him or her.

In that moment I truly became a mom.

I'd never been a very religious person, but at that moment I knew there was some God somewhere that allowed miracles like this to happen, and I silently thanked him for letting one happen to me.

I looked over at my husband; his eyes were glassy, a goofy smile etched on his face.

Our baby was finally real.

CHAPTER THREE

I dreaded telling our families about my pregnancy. My family had been bombarding me with "the baby question" for almost four years, but for some reason, at the age of thirty-two, I still felt a little naughty telling my parents that I was knocked up. It was a confirmation to my parents that I really was having sex. I had spent a big portion of my life trying to hide my sex life, and now I was supposed to suddenly make it common knowledge?

I was hesitant to tell my husband's family because, quite frankly, they annoyed me, and I knew we would never hear the end of it. Chris is an only child, and I'm pretty sure his mother had dreamt of being a grandma since her son was old enough to walk. I hated the thought of having to model my blossoming bump for them over Skype.

I absolutely loved the fact that Chris and I, with the exception of our doctors, were the only ones who knew about this little miracle coming our way. It brought us closer together. It felt so thrilling, like having your first kiss every day. Sharing our most intimate secret with other people somehow took some of the magic away.

As I entered my second trimester, my belly began to protrude, and my husband confronted me with the inevitable.

"You know, we're going to have to tell people eventually," he said. "We can't keep this a secret forever."

I thought for a minute. Our families were both significant distances away. If we tried hard enough, it was feasible that we could go right up until my delivery before we told anyone.

I didn't have a problem telling our friends—I was sure half of them knew anyway based on the simple fact that we'd stopped going out as much, and when we did I sipped on water or Sprite. But telling our families was, well, it was just different.

I was about to swear Chris to eternal secrecy when he spoke. "We'll do it whenever you're ready."

The guilt rushed in. He trusted me with this monumental decision, and I was being selfish and immature. As much as I wanted the pregnancy to be all about us, I knew it wasn't. Babies are supposed to be shared.

We were a few weeks into the second trimester, and, based on everything I'd read, well into the "safe zone." I reluctantly supposed it was time to let it out. We settled on telling our families over the upcoming weekend, and I held tightly to my last few days of privacy. That Saturday I called my older brother, then my parents. Chris called his parents last.

Once the secret was out, it was overwhelming. We were faced with a firing squad of questions from every direction. Word traveled across the family trees like a lightning bolt, and our phone rang off the hook. "Have you thought of names?" "What do you think it is?" "Do you want a boy or a girl?" "Do you have the nursery ready?" "Have you felt the baby move?" "Where are you going to have your shower?" "Are you going to have people in the delivery room?" The questions went on and on and on.

I was only a third of the way through my pregnancy—I was supposed to have a nursery ready? I hadn't bought anything. Was I behind? Where was the manual that told me all of this stuff? My old friend fear rushed back to greet me, and I resumed questioning my ability to be a mother. Here I was, just sitting around, happy as a clam, letting precious time pass as my baby grew and grew. I didn't realize I was doing everything wrong. I needed to shop, to prepare, to get ready. But I didn't really feel like it. Did that make me a horrible person, a terrible mother-to-be? Maybe I wasn't cut out to have a baby. Was it too late to change my mind?

From the second my pregnancy became public, it seemed everyone's personal information filter was ripped off. Coworkers I barely knew asked if I would breastfeed. The clerk at the grocery store asked if I was going to have my baby "naturally." I was amazed how a simple baby bump made complete strangers think it was appropriate to ask random questions about my breasts and vagina.

Each time someone inquired about my uterus, whether friend, family, or stranger, I politely answered the question, even though I usually wanted to tell them to mind their own damn business. Then I took a deep breath, smiled, and remembered ever so clearly why I wanted to keep the baby our little secret in the first place.

The weeks flew by, and even though people were driving me crazy, it became clear that I was having "The Perfect Pregnancy." Aside from being annoyed by inquisitive relatives, I had very little to complain about. I was a little tired and my blood pressure was "high normal," but other than that, things were great. I exercised daily, ate like a queen, and was genuinely happy. And while it took a while, by the time I reached the halfway point of my pregnancy, I was finally getting used to the idea of having a baby.

Twenty weeks brought the gender ultrasound. Hearing the heartbeat for the first time had made my baby real, but seeing my child on a screen not only made me love my baby even more, it gave me a glimpse into my future. Our future.

There was never a question in my mind that we were going to learn the sex of the baby. People often asked what my mother's intuition told me; I truly had no clue, and I honestly didn't think I had a preference. I was a tomboy with some girly-girl mixed in, so I figured either one would make me happy.

Chris, on the other hand, was certain the baby was a girl. "Payback for my younger years," he liked to joke.

As we entered the dimly lit ultrasound room, my body twitched with excitement. I climbed on the table and took a deep breath, anxious for the big reveal. In an instant, Chris and I saw our child on the screen. He or she was only the size of a banana, but we could see everything clear as day. As the technician moved her device across my belly, I watched as a tiny human did flips right in front of me, amazed at the acrobatics going on inside.

"Did you feel that?" the tech asked, smiling.

"No," I replied. "Was I supposed to feel something?"

She shrugged. "It just looked like the baby kicked you pretty hard, but maybe not."

I hadn't felt much movement, a flutter here and there, but I'd heard that it takes first-time moms longer to feel the baby. Now, watching this baby flip and kick on the screen and not feeling a thing, I was beginning to wonder if I had a uterus of steel.

Our child continued to dance back and forth in front of us, putting on a show for its first audience. I smiled as a tiny hand waved hello and couldn't help but wonder if our baby knew we were watching.

The technician focused in on a throbbing ball in our baby's chest.

"This is the heart," she said. "It's beating nicely. Blood flow looks good."

She went through the major organs one by one, explaining what each was.

"Well, everything looks great. You've got a healthy baby." The tech smiled, lifting the wand from my abdomen. "Did you guys want to know the sex?"

I was so entranced with the magic happening onscreen that I'd almost forgotten.

"Yes," Chris and I answered in unison.

The technician rolled the device back over my belly and zoomed in between the baby's legs. She drew an arrow and typed "It's a girl!" on the screen.

"I knew it," Chris gasped, feigning disappointment. But I could tell he could barely contain his excitement. Our baby already had Daddy wrapped around her tiny little finger.

"Girls are so much fun," the woman smiled, wiping the extra jelly from my stomach.

I hadn't realized it, but I'd wanted a girl all along. Even though I should have been basking in the fact that my baby was healthy, I was completely focused on the fact that I was going to have a daughter. My daughter. I couldn't help but imagine the future, a pretty little girl playing dress-up in my heels, falling in love for the first time, her first heartbreak, choosing a prom dress, choosing a wedding dress. Would she be blond and fair like me, or dark like her father? I stared at the ultrasound pictures, trying to tell from the black-and-white prints. I couldn't wait to meet her face to face.

"Are you excited?" Chris asked as we left the office.

"Yes," I answered, grinning sheepishly. "Are you?"

"Of course I am. I would have been excited either way." My husband studied my face, his eyes narrowing. "You wanted a girl all along, didn't you?"

"I would have been happy either way," I mimicked. But we both knew the truth.

I started my car and watched my husband drive off, headed back to work. I had the day off but wasn't ready to go home. I hadn't purchased anything for our baby, but now that I knew it was a girl, I felt she needed something to hang in her closet. I tried to tell myself it was for her, when really I just wanted something tangible to remind me of the sweet baby girl growing in my belly. I headed to Old Navy, where I browsed the baby section with a stupid grin, stifling the urge to announce to my fellow shoppers I was having a girl.

I'd never spent much time looking for baby clothes and was elated by the cuteness of everything I touched. The ruffles, the eyelets, the bows—they all made me feel warm and fuzzy. My little girl would be born in July, and I spent close to an hour fixated on a rack of tiny sundresses. They had purple, pink, white, yellow, flowered, striped…so many to choose from. It was her first purchase, so it had to be perfect. I finally settled on a white cotton dress with purple flowers and a ruffled hem.

I drove home in a giddy haze, counting the days until I could put that adorable dress on my baby girl.

CHAPTER FOUR

We decided to name her Avery.

Years before we talked about having children, I was getting ready for the start of the school year. I looked at a stack of labels and saw the name "Avery" stamped on the back. I thought it was a beautiful name, so I solicited my husband's opinion.

"Do you like the name Avery?"

"Why, are you pregnant?" he joked.

"No, I just think it's a pretty name. I think it would be a good girl's name. If it's even a name that you name people."

"I like it."

"Me too."

Two years later, we unanimously decided to name our daughter after an office supply company.

*****

After the excitement of finding out the baby's sex faded, life pretty much went back to normal, except now I knew a little more about the person growing inside of me. Every night before bed I asked God to keep my baby girl healthy. I made up the "Avery Song," which I sang every morning in the shower. (Avery, Avery, sweetest little girl that ever would be…) I'd drive to work every morning listening to Colbie Caillat's "Capri"—a song about a woman pregnant with a baby girl—and cry happy tears. In the evenings I'd play Mozart on my baby grand Kawai, hoping the music would jump-start my daughter's intelligence.

Every time I went to the store, whether it was Target, Macy's, or the grocery story, I had to pick up something for Avery. On weekend mornings Chris and I lounged in bed for hours poking at my belly, waiting to feel our daughter's soft kicks and gasping with delight when we saw my stomach roll.

My belly grew rapidly, and we had one more sonogram before a much-needed spring break trip to San Jose Del Cabo, Mexico, just to make sure I wouldn't, at twenty-six weeks, go into labor in a foreign country. The pictures weren't great, but I was assured everything looked fine, and my doctor provided a list of things to avoid. We had spent countless vacations in Mexico, and, though a few skeptics questioned the safety of our vacation destination, I was ready to unwind.

Chris and I spent a glorious week in a beachside condo, remembering who we were before a baby came into our lives and submerging ourselves in pure, simple relaxation. Each morning I watched the sun rise, shamelessly donned a bikini, and did laps around the deserted pool, my heavy belly weightless in the sparkling blue water. Avery was also an early riser, and as I floated peacefully I could feel her swimming in her own temperate pool, practicing flutter kicks and backstrokes in the sunshine.

We read books by the ocean, took naps in the shade, and held hands like smitten teenagers as we walked on the beach. In the evenings I'd slip into a sundress and we'd go to a fine restaurant, savoring dishes like chipotle-glazed sea scallops and hot pepper fudge cake. We strolled through the squares of the quaint little Mexican town like newlyweds, sharing the news of our precious daughter with all who asked.

We returned to our condo in time to watch the sunset, sitting in wind-worn Adirondack chairs facing the ocean, my husband enjoying a Dos Equis while I sipped a glass of lemonade. Before bed, Chris would slather my tummy in cocoa butter and talk to our daughter. "When are you going to get here?" he'd ask. "We can't wait to meet you."

During that week I fell more in love with my husband and my daughter. It was a glorious seven days of harmony, where for a brief stitch in time all was right with the world. Looking back on that perfect week, it was the last time I felt completely at peace.

*****

If you ask a woman who has carried a baby to term, she'll probably tell you the first thirty weeks go by quickly. The next ten, not so much.

The weeks following our vacation, I grew bigger and more uncomfortable and, with the rising temperatures and humidity of a late Midwestern spring, very bloated. As a teacher I was on my feet all day; cankles became part of life. Colleagues constantly commented on my puffiness. Students asked if I was going to give birth in class because I was "huge" and "ready to pop." My ass barely fit on a toilet seat, which was unfortunate because I had to sit on it every five minutes and pee. My back ached, my disposition soured, and I was counting the days until the school year ended and I could spend my days on the couch.

The bigger I became the less Avery moved, which made me nervous, but my doctors, as well as every pregnancy book, reassured me this was normal. It was my first pregnancy, so I didn't have anything to compare her to besides other people's pregnancy stories. She had always been somewhat quiet, and, since everything always looked fine when I went to the doctor, I told myself that my daughter was just a very polite little girl.

As time wore on, however, I became increasingly paranoid. Hours would go by with no movement, and I would start to panic. But every time I worked myself up enough to actually call the doctor, Avery would give me a little kick here, a little punch there, a little "Hi, Mom," to let me know that everything was okay, and my mind would ease once again.

Summer vacation officially began, and I was flat-out miserable. For the first few weeks I tromped from baby shower to baby shower, where I received enough pink onesies to clothe a small country of newborns. Women I barely knew rubbed my belly and shared with me the perils of motherhood. Grandmas gave me knowing smiles and insisted a little whiskey would be good for teething. I smiled and played along, but I didn't want to be at a party, even if it was for me. I was fat, swollen, and exhausted; my idea of a good time was napping on the couch, and even that was becoming a chore.

The only solace I found was on our boat, a little yellow skiboat lovingly nicknamed "The Big Banana." While in Cabo we'd purchased a decal for it that read NO BAD DAYS, and it was close to impossible to be miserable out on the water. Chris and I would take the boat out each weekend, where I would float around on a purple noodle feeling blessedly buoyant, my swollen body shrinking in the cool, crisp water of Gull Lake. If I felt daring, I'd lift up my maternity suit and tan my massive abdomen, feeling my daughter twist and turn under the warmth of the sun's rays. Ironically, the time I spent in the water was the only time I didn't feel like a whale.

After a while, though, even the boat began to irritate me. I was tired of my husband freely sipping cocktails while I chugged water in the hot sun to avoid dehydration. I was tired of having to pee because I drank so much water. I was tired of trying to get my fat ass in and out of the boat, frightened I would trip and hurt Avery. I was tired of worrying my water might break while floating in the lake and I wouldn't notice, leading to a nasty infection that would hurt my baby. I was tired of being paranoid. I was tired of being enormous and pregnant. But most of all, I was just tired of being tired.

For the first eight months, I had managed to avoid becoming the "crazy pregnant woman" our male friends had warned my husband I would inevitably become. Chris would laugh and say that wouldn't happen to his wife, not his awesome, low-maintenance, fun-loving, beer-drinking wife, and I was proud because I thought it was true.

Then the ninth month came.

Out of nowhere I was bitter at the world and pissed at Chris for his lack of sacrifice, for not having to change his life one bit, even though I knew that his life had changed. I was pissed at Avery for making me change mine, and I was pissed at myself for being selfish enough to be pissed at my loving husband and unborn daughter. I also felt intense guilt. I was supposed to be focused on my baby. I was supposed to be filled with excitement that the tiny little person I'd cared for and loved inside of me for what seemed like an eternity was finally weeks, maybe even days away from making her grand entrance into the world. Instead, I kept thinking of all of the things I wouldn't be able to do once she arrived. I felt like a terrible person, and a terrible mother.

I remember it like it was yesterday; it still makes me cringe. I was thirty-seven and a half weeks pregnant. It was a warm Sunday afternoon, June 29, 2008, to be exact. We were relaxing on the Big Banana, just like we did every Sunday afternoon. I was in the front reading a parenting magazine, unable to concentrate and disgusted that I was bulging out of my maternity suit. Chris sat in the captain's chair, drinking a Miller Lite and fiddling with the radio.

I'm not exactly sure what he said to ignite me, but I exploded like an illegal firework.

"It's not fair. You get to do whatever the fuck you want while I'm going to be stuck at home with a baby stuck to my boob, carrying her around and cleaning up shit twenty-four hours a day," I screamed. "I get to be fat and disgusting and tired, and you just get to have your life stay the same. I hate this."

My husband stared at me as I fought back the tears. I was usually the levelheaded one who controlled my feelings, and this caught him off guard.

"Do you really think that? That I'm just going to run off and leave you home alone with the baby?" he started slowly, containing his anger. "Thanks for having a lot of faith in me."

In truth, I really believed my husband would continue to be a wonderful husband and an even better father. My resentment wasn't resentment at all, but fear, and it was easier for me to get angry than to admit I was terrified of so many things. I was scared of physically giving birth, that it might hurt too much or

I somehow wouldn't do it right. Motherhood was knocking at my door, and I was worried that I wasn't ready to let it in, that I didn't know how to be the "perfect" mother. Most of all, I was afraid of the unknown.

I wanted to cry but held it in. I longed to tearfully leap into my husband's arms, to have him hold me and stroke my hair and tell me that everything was going to be okay, that I was beautiful and wonderful and Avery was the luckiest baby in the world to have a mother like me. Instead I did what I do best. I took a deep breath, shoved my emotions back down, picked up my magazine, and turned around.

CHAPTER FIVE

Monday morning came bright and too early, as it tends to, except for once I didn't have to get up and go to work.Chris gave me a kiss goodbye as I curled my enormous belly up against his vacant pillow. I noticed my fingers; I hadn't even gotten out of bed yet and they looked like tiny cocktail sausages.

"We need to put that car seat in," I murmured drowsily. We'd been meaning to do it for a few weeks, but life kept getting in the way. "I don't want to be unprepared."

"I'll do it tonight or tomorrow," my husband replied, putting on his watch."Get some rest."

My hormonal temper tantrum had passed, and I was back to being my normal self. I was still scared—aren't all new mothers?—but I no longer hated my husband, and the excitement of Avery's pending arrival had returned.

It was a normal day. I showered, ate breakfast, watched *The View*, and went to Target. I took a walk around the neighborhood, enjoying the gorgeous sunshine of the last day of June. I ate a grilled cheese and tomato sandwich with a hearty helping of strawberries. Avery loved strawberries; I joked that she would come out with red hair since she made me eat a quart every day.

By midafternoon I was exhausted and curled up on the couch to do my kick counts. Avery was quiet, so I drank a glass of juice to get her moving. Before long I felt a few small movements—pretty standard for her—and then she was done. I refused to worry, for this was the dance we had been doing for weeks. Besides, I had just been to the doctor forty-eight hours earlier, and he assured me everything looked fine.

I fell asleep, my arms cradling my daughter.

I woke an hour later to an uncomfortable pressure on my pelvis. As I stood, the pain worsened; for a second it was borderline excruciating, and then it was gone. I went to the bathroom to pee. As I stood to flush I noticed something strange in the toilet, and my mind raced back to our birthing class. It was my mucus plug.

Oh my God, I thought, adrenaline coursing through my body. It's finally happening. I'm going into labor soon. All of the fear I had experienced dissolved in an instant, and my heart began to race with excitement. I took a deep breath and smiled. After thirty-eight long weeks, I was finally going to meet my daughter.

The next few hours were anticlimactic as I anxiously waited for something to happen. The pain in my pelvis continued to come and go, but there were no contractions. It can take days for labor to start after losing the mucus plug, but for some reason I knew it was time. My mother's intuition was telling me it was time.

Chris came home from work; together we waited.

And waited.

And waited.

Nothing happened.

I had joked for months that Avery's lease on my uterus was up at the end of June so she needed to find a new place to live. The final day of the month was almost over, and it appeared she was staying put.

I went to bed with a baby still in my belly.

I awoke to darkness two hours later, feeling a warm pop between my legs. It was like nothing I'd ever felt; it had to be my water breaking. I glanced at the clock—12:20 a.m.—and then at my husband, peacefullyasleep.

"Honey," I whispered. My words were met with heavy breathing. "Honey," I repeated, a little louder this time, tapping him on the shoulder.

"Hmmmmm…." he groaned, still not quite awake.

"I think my water just broke."

"What?" he shouted, tossing back the covers and scrambling to his feet. I switched on my bedside lamp.

"I think my…." The words escaped me as I stood up. Fluid poured from my loins, but not the clear, watery fluid we'd discussed in birthing class. It was the dark, sticky flush of fresh blood. Something was wrong.

"Oh my God, oh my God…" I repeated, paralyzed. I didn't know what to do, what to say. I stood shaking, chanting those words, blood pouring from my crotch, painting the cream carpeting crimson.

"Does it hurt?" Chris asked, frantically pulling on his clothes.

I didn't know if it hurt; I couldn't feel anything. The only thing I could feel was that something was wrong.

He grabbed my arm and led me to the bathroom, dark splatters trailing my footsteps. There was so much blood; I thought I might pass out.

"Get in the shower, I'll call the doctor," he demanded.

I stood mute under the hot water, a terrified little girl with my heart in my stomach, waiting for someone to tell me what to do, waiting for someone to tell me everything was going to be okay.

The cramped walls of the shower closed in on me. I felt sick as I grasped the slippery tile with my left hand. I thought I was going to die; I thought Avery was going to die.

My husband reappeared. "I talked to the doctor, he said to come in now," he breathed, rushing around, grabbing my things. "The doctors are going to take care of you. It's going to be okay."

He helped me out of the shower. I was shaking uncontrollably, blood and fluid flowing freely from my vagina. As he dried me off, a large red puddle appeared on the floor.

"Oh my God," I howled.

"They're going to take care of you," Chris repeated, grabbing my shoulders and looking me in the eye. "Everything is going to be okay."

He said it so many times I started to believe him.

It took another ten minutes to leave the house; I was wearing half a package of maxi-pads between my legs, but by the time we tried to get out the door, they were soaked through. Finally, after my third pair of pants, we stuffed two towels between my legs and got in the car.

We made it down the driveway when my husband slammed the car back into park. "Shit," he breathed, running back into the house.

He emerged with the car seat, tossing it into the back of our SUV. I couldn't help but smile. We were going to have a baby, after all. Everything was going to be okay.

It had to be.

The hospital was a fifteen-minute drive from our house. On a normal day it was a relaxing, scenic drive through the country, full of cornfields and horse pastures and all things nature. But that night it was excruciating. Chris sped along the winding roads, but it still felt like we were moving in slow motion.

"Are you okay? Does it hurt?" he asked as we drove.

Physically I felt fine, but mentally I was reeling. I stared bleary-eyed at the lights of the houses we passed, hazy beams through the warm, humid night air. I imagined the happy, sleeping families inside, oblivious to my life, ignorant of the happenings outside their windows.

"Everything is going to be okay, right?" I pleaded, more to God than to my husband. "That's what doctors do, they fix things. They perform miracles."

By the time we reached the hospital, our dread was replaced with hope; my husband and I truly believed we'd be leaving the hospital with our baby girl in our arms.

The night clerk met me at the door with a wheelchair. She was in no hurry, making small talk about how busy they were that evening. "I'm surprised it's not a full moon!" she giggled. "Because that myth is true, ya know."

My husband and I, always the well-mannered couple, met her chatter with weak smiles and forced laughter. "Hurry up!"

I shouted internally. "Don't you realize something is wrong with my baby?" I looked over at Chris, and I could tell our thoughts matched.

We were taken upstairs to the triage area, where two scrub-clad nurses waited. They smiled at us as we rolled into the small curtained area, finishing up a conversation about something amusing and trivial like *The Bachelor* or *American Idol*.

"All right," said the blond nurse, the older of the two. "I need you to take off your pants and your underwear and get up on the table." I stayed seated in the wheelchair, afraid to stand up. I looked dumbly at Chris, hoping he could find the words that escaped me.

He looked at the nurses, exasperation crossing his face. We both were confused by how normal everyone was acting, simply going about their business with no sense of urgency. While it frustrated my husband, it relaxed me. I became increasingly confident that what was happening to me was somehow normal. I'd never had a baby before; perhaps I was overreacting.

"There's a lot of blood when she stands up," Chris managed.

The blond nurse smiled. "Okay, that can be normal. But we need to get you up here so we can examine you and see how far along you are."

I reluctantly stood from the chair and began stripping off my bottoms; blood and fluid gushed out, soiling my already stained pajama pants, finally ending in a murky puddle on the beige tile floor. The nurses, once relaxed and jovial, became flustered.

"Oh my," the brunette breathed, rushing to grab my arm. "Oh my. Are you in any pain? Are you dizzy?"

"I feel fine," I whined helplessly. "I just want to know what's wrong."

"Get the ultrasound machine," Blond Nurse directed her partner. "And find the doctor, *now*."

I made it up on the table, terrified now that things seemed more serious, but nonetheless embarrassed for the mess I was making. Damn my mother for giving me impeccable manners.

"Did you have a fall?" the nurse inquired, glancing quickly at Chris. Was she really suggesting that my husband was responsible?

I looked the nurse in the eye as I answered. "No. We were sleeping, my water broke, I got up, and there was all this blood."

"Have you been using any illegal drugs? Cocaine?"

"No." I laughed bitterly. Did this woman seriously think we were drug addicts—my husband in his striped polo shirt and khaki shorts, me in my sorority sweatshirt and glasses? "We don't use drugs."

"I had to ask; those are standard questions in a situation like this," she explained, putting on surgical gloves.

Blond Nurse examined my pelvis first. "You're only dilated to a one. Let's see if I can get a heartbeat."

"Can get a heartbeat"? I thought. Why wouldn't she be able to get a heartbeat? My daughter had a good, strong heartbeat. That's what the doctors always said. She was healthy as a horse— why wouldn't they be able to find it?

I looked at my husband, my rock. Holding my hand, he smiled. "It's going to be okay," he choked. His words were thick and choppy and clung to his throat.

Brunette Nurse returned as her partner brought out the fetal Doppler.

"The doctor will be here in a minute," she promised, putting her hand on my shoulder.

"All right, let's take a listen," said Blond Nurse.

We held our breath in unison and prayed as the Doppler traveled across my stomach. I expected to hear the strong, solid pounding of my baby girl's heart. I had heard it just seventy-two hours before.

Since the first time Avery's tiny heart was shared with the world, it had always been easy for the doctors to find, usually showing up within seconds. The nurse had been trying for a full minute, and all we heard was the *whoosh whoosh* of my insides. I felt a wave of nausea rush over me. A thousand tiny thorns pricked my skin, and I feared blacking out. Chris squeezed my hand tighter.

"She could be at a weird angle, let me try again," the nurse sputtered, feverishly rubbing the machine back and forth across my abdomen.

Clop-clop. Clop-clop. Finally, after an eternity of waiting, we heard the sweet sound off in the distance.

"That's it," my husband announced with excitement. "That's her."

I breathed a sigh of relief and started laughing. That silly Avery, playing a trick on us. We both looked at the nurse, expecting her to share our elation.

Blond Nurse had tears in her eyes and looked like she might vomit.

"I'm so sorry," she whispered softly. "That's your heart."

*****

"This sucks," Brunette Nurse breathed, pacing. "This really does."

"The doctor will be here with the ultrasound in a minute," Blond Nurse sighed. "We'll know more then."

The nurses stood fidgeting in uncomfortable silence. It seemed like hours, but only fifteen minutes had passed since we'd arrived at the hospital door.

The doctor finally made his entrance, wheeling a small machine into my makeshift room.

"All right," he said matter-of-factly. "Let's see what the problem is."

He was short and graying, one of the three doctors in the practice. He'd examined me a handful of times, and I liked him well enough.

"Have you had prenatal care during your pregnancy?" he inquired, readying the ultrasound machine.

I stared at him blankly, in disbelief. I knew they were a busy practice, but did he really ask that question? I stared at him again, hoping he would recognize me and admit his mistake.

He stared back as if I were a complete stranger, a person off the street, a crack whore in a Delta Gamma sweatshirt who had wandered into the hospital looking for a fix. Yet I still gave him the benefit of the doubt—I probably looked different with no makeup, wearing my glasses. But he should've recognized Chris...

"Yes," I said steadily. "I just saw one of your partners Friday. Her heartbeat was a little faster than usual, but it was still normal. He said everything was fine." I had the sudden urge to slap the doctor I had seen last, who told me she was "fine." Her heartbeat was a little faster—why didn't he look into it? Avery obviously wasn't "fine."

The doctor studied my face, trying to place me.I began to feel guilty, like I was hiding something, like I had done something wrong. Had I?

"When was the last time you felt your baby move?"he asked.

"This morning," I answered, searching my memory. I'd been doing my kick counts, but Avery was never very predictable. "Early this morning, before I got up. And I think a little this afternoon, too....She hasn't been moving much, but she's never been a mover. Everyone told me that was normal..."

"It can be normal," he stated dryly, squirting warm jelly on my stomach.

He ran the machine across my belly. Avery was instantly visible, curled up in a little ball inside of me. It had been over two months since my last ultrasound; I was amazed at how much she'd grown.

"There she is." I smiled, looking to my husband. For some reason I felt better, as if the fact that she was still in there made everything okay. It was silly, really—where would she have gone? It was obvious by looking at me she was still in there, but for a split second I felt relief.

Chris looked at me, forcing a smile. "That's our girl," he whispered.

We turned to the doctor, silently awaiting an explanation.

"Okay," he started, taking a deep breath, like the words he was about to speak required more air than normal words. "Okay. That's your baby's heart." He pointed to a nickel-sized spot on the screen. "The problem is, it's not beating. I'm sorry."

A palpable silence filled the room. I looked from the doctor to the nurses; their faces were so serious. I turned to the left, to my husband, who had released my hand for the first time that night.

"That's it?" Chris asked, his voice barely audible.

We both expected a solution, to be whisked down the hall *Gray's Anatomy*–style, where a team of highly specialized doctors would take time away from their messy love lives to work magic on my unborn baby. But we just sat there and stared at each other, the hum of the florescent hospital lights blaring through the silence.

"I'm sorry," the doctor repeated.

Chris struggled to regain his composure, the color completely drained from his tan Italian skin. "But why?" he pleaded. "How?"

"Stillbirths are fairly common. Around one out of every one hundred babies," he said, sending chills down my spine.

Fairly common? I thought. Then why the hell didn't any-one ever tell me this was a possibility? The doctors hadn't mentioned it; the books hadn't mentioned it. I'd been lied to my entire pregnancy.

I wanted my happy ending.

"We'll know more after we get the baby out," he continued. "From the blood I'd think a placental abruption, which could be caused by a number of things, like a pretty traumatic fall or using drugs. But you're saying neither of those happened. Plus you're not in any pain, which you would be with an abruption. We'll figure it out." He turned and walked away, stopping to whisper to the nurses as he pulled the curtain back.

Chris and I were alone. I turned to my husband, making a sorry attempt at a smile. I was the funny one, the one who cracked jokes in times of darkness. But this darkness was unfamiliar territory. I couldn't find any words, and I watched powerlessly as Chris's head fell into his hands, his strong body shaking with grief. He let out a wretched groan and burst into tears. I reached for his trembling hand and watched silently as my rock began to crumble.

I, on the other hand, couldn't process my grief. While my husband was sobbing, fighting the urge to punch someone or something, I sat completely still, emotionless. I nodded my head over and over, as if someone were still speaking to me in the silent room. I was numb; no tears filled my eyes, no choked sobs escaped my chest. In my mind there was a different woman lying in that bed, a woman who looked like me but wasn't quite.

I watched that stranger react to the news that the baby girl she had carried in her womb for just shy of nine months was lying dead inside of her. The woman cried, screamed and flailed, clawed at the nurses, took blind swings at the doctor, the evil man who'd just delivered the most devastating news of her thirty-two years. She howled like a rabid animal, kicking and biting and knocking over expensive equipment, oblivious to everything but her own pain. "Why, why, why?" she sobbed, as men in white rushed to restrain her.

I lay motionless on that hospital bed, soaked in my own blood, my hands folded over the belly that had become a tomb, thinking of that woman, the woman who raged in my head, the woman I was but couldn't be.

CHAPTER SIX

When I was twenty-one, I had my palm read outside of a bar. My friends and I were on our way in to have a few drinks and, since it was only five bucks, we thought it would be fun. The middle-aged woman made us laugh in her glittery purple silk robe and matching eyeshadow. A shiny red scarf covered her greasy black hair; it fluttered around her slim shoulders as she traced the lines of my hand with her long, bony fingers.

"I see a long life with much happiness," she began, forcing a terrible Eastern European accent. "Yes, much happiness, but also…"

The woman paused and looked at me, frowning.

"What?" I laughed nervously, curious to know what made her stop.

She sucked in a deep breath and pushed it out slowly with her tongue, her talons still moving methodically across my hand. She smelled of stale cigarettes and peppermint.

"Right there," she breathed, pointing to a line on my left hand. She leaned in closer, whispering in my ear. "Have you had a miscarriage?"

I let out a short laugh, taken aback by her bluntness. "Uh, no," I replied slowly, shooting my friends a look that shouted this woman was crazy. I was a twenty-one-year-old college student. Kids and miscarriages were the last thing on my mind.

The gypsy stared at me, frowning. "I am very sorry, but I see on your hand the loss of a child. I am very sorry," she repeated, calmly shaking her head from left to right before erupting into a big, toothy smile. "But after that, a long happy life."

I walked into the bar a little flustered but quickly forgot the strange woman's words. I don't know if it was magic or bad luck, but eleven years later, I was forced to remember them all too clearly.

*****

We finally settled into our hospital room at around two a.m. They placed us in the bariatric room, a larger room meant for bigger mothers secluded from the rest of the maternity ward. I'm not obese, but it was the only room that had its own wing. It was nice of them, I suppose, saving me the grief of having to be near other pregnant women, women experiencing the joyous miracle of birth the right way. I doubt they wanted any pregnant women to be near me, either, as Chris and I were enveloped in an easily recognizable cloud of despair.

Chris crawled into my bed and wrapped his arms around me, afraid to let go. It reminded me of the scene in *Titanic* where the old couple, trapped in the hollows of the sinking ship, lie in bed together and hold each other tightly, waiting to take their inevitable final breaths.

That was us, holding on to each other because there wasn't anything else we could do. Letting go would mean facing our reality alone, and we would die if we were forced to do that. I was in shock and had yet to cry, but the magnitude of what had happened was slowly sinking in.

"I still have to deliver this baby," I sputtered, sickened by the reality of the situation. "How the hell am I supposed to deliver this baby? Can't they just cut it out?" For a moment Avery was no longer my daughter, no longer my sweet baby girl. She was just this thing I had to get out of me. I had a dead baby floating around in my belly, a carcass, and it was disgusting.

"I don't know," Chris replied, his grief replaced with anger. "It would be nice if someone would tell us what was going on."

We sat alone in our room for thirty minutes before we saw anyone else. I assume we were being given a chance to process what was happening, but we weren't ready to grieve. We wanted a solution. We had a problem; our baby was dead. We understood that, at least as best we could given the suddenness of the situation. How were we going to fix our problem? How were they going to fix it?

In my mind it was simple: Cut her out and send me home so I could forget this pregnancy ever happened.

Problem solved.

A young nurse finally appeared at the door. (As with all of the many nurses I met during my hospital stay, the names are hazy, but I'll call her Julia.)

Julia was chubby in a healthy way. She had a beautiful, sweet face, accentuated by a pile of wavy auburn hair tied into a loose bun at the top of her head. A sad smile graced her lips, and she radiated genuine empathy.

"How are you guys doing?" she asked softly, not waiting for an answer before starting again. "I know that's a stupid question. But I mean, given everything, are you feeling okay? Is there anything you need? Anything I can get you?"

A live baby would be nice.

"We're fine, thanks," Chris and I both answered bitterly. Our version of *fine* was quite different from most people's at that moment. Saying we were fine meant that we weren't in unbearable physical pain and weren't contemplating suicide in the near future.

Julia pulled a stool close to my bed. "Okay. There's a lot of things we need to go over, if you're up for it," she said softly. "Or if not, I can come back later."

Chris and I agreed there was no time like the present.

"Okay, first I need to ask you a few questions," she continued, glancing at my husband. "Is there any violence in your relationship?"

A tired laugh escaped my throat. Chris and I rarely argued.

"No, no violence."

The young woman smiled apologetically. "Sorry, but I have to ask these questions. Any illegal drug use during your pregnancy?"

"Nope."

"Alcohol?"

"Nope."

"Smoking?"

"Nope."

"Were you seeing an OBGYN for your entire pregnancy?"

"Yep."

I could see the irritation building in Chris. While her tone was far from accusatory, it felt like we were being blamed for what happened to Avery, as if the medical community was saying her death couldn't possibly have been an accident.

"Listen," Chris said, clenching his fists and relaxing them again. "We did everything by the book. We did everything right. The doctors said Heidi had a perfect pregnancy."

The nurse gave a nod of understanding. "You two don't look like the type to be into drugs, but you never know. I have to ask, it's standard protocol," she replied.

I flashed a weak smile.

"We get it," Chris murmured.

I understood the inquisition was procedure, but it made me feel guilty, and I couldn't shake the idea that Avery's death was somehow my fault.

"Okay. So we're waiting to do one more ultrasound with the best machine we have just to confirm the situation…" She stopped. "I'm so sorry, but we have to be sure. We're also going to take a bunch of blood from you and pretty much run every test imaginable to try to find out why this happened and make sure it's not something that could happen again."

Happen again? Why was she talking about the future? I didn't care about the future. I had a dead baby trapped in my uterus. What I needed was for someone to tell when that was going to end.

"So that's where we are right now." She smiled. "There are a lot of things we still need to go over, but I'll be back to talk about those. I'll be here all night, so please, please, please call for me if you need anything."

As Julia turned to go, a small woman in scrubs entered the room pushing a machine straight out of *Star Trek*.

"I'm here to do one more ultrasound, with this machine," she explained, all business.

So this was the super machine, the granddaddy of them all. This was the last hope of finding any sign of life left in my daughter.

My emotional pendulum swung from despair back to hope as my belly was again slathered with gel for Avery's final ultrasound. No one spoke; no one breathed. The picture on this machine was better, clearer, larger. And it was just as disappointing.

Avery was exactly where she had been on the last ultrasound, and her heart was just as still.

"I'm very sorry," the woman offered, pushing the machine out of the room. "I really am."

"Thank you," I whispered, forcing another half-hearted smile. It hurt me to cause other people, even strangers, so much sadness.

Chris climbed back on the bed and gave me a kiss, placing his hand on my belly.

"So now what do we do?" he asked, stroking my hair.

There was so much to do, but I was confined to the room. We needed to tell our parents, our friends...but it was the middle of the night. Besides, what would we say? "Hi, Mom, Avery's dead." I didn't think I'd even be able to say the words out loud. Outside of the hospital, we were the only ones in the world who knew where we were at that moment, and part of me wanted to keep it that way. It was going to hurt too bad sharing the news; it was going to hurt too bad sharing the pain.

"I have to pee," I replied, heaving myself up and placing my swollen feet on the floor. The cold tile felt good on my feet; it sent a chill up my back that reminded me I was still alive.

As Chris grabbed my arm to help steady me, more fluid poured onto the floor. More fluid and more blood.

"Oh God, why won't it stop?" I moaned. I glanced at the bed; it was soaked in brown liquid. I looked down at myself, at my filthy blue hospital gown covered in stains. I hadn't realized I was still gushing. "I'm making such a mess."

"Don't worry about it," my husband said, helping me to the toilet. A trail of murky wetness followed me into the bathroom. "I'll call the nurse."

Julia immediately appeared. "Is everything okay?" she asked.

Chris looked worried. "She's still losing a lot of fluid and there's still a lot of blood. Is that normal?"

The nurse stepped deeper into the room, looking around at my mess. "That is a lot," she said. "But it's still pretty normal. Let me know if it doesn't slow down, though. I'll get you some pads for the bed. I'll get you a few gowns, too, and I'll have someone come and clean the floor for you. Do you guys want something to drink? Water? Sprite?"

"Oh, Sprite would be heavenly," I said, realizing I was parched. "A Sprite and a water, if you could. Thank you so much."

"My pleasure."

I looked out the window and sipped my Sprite as Chris placed fresh blue absorbent pads on my bed and an orderly mopped the floor. It was close to three a.m., and the streets were still swaddled in their dark slumber. Every now and then a car passed by, someone going somewhere for some reason. People living their lives—happy people, probably—while I was prisoner of a hospital room, trapped in my own nightmare. For a second I had the impulse to leave, to run out the hospital doors and not look back, to never see any of these people ever again.

A phlebotomist entered the room as I crawled back into bed, yearning to escape.

"Hi there," she said, her voice gruff and manly. "I'm here to draw some blood?" The woman was young with boxed black hair and a pierced nose and lip. She began to chat about working the night shift, and it quickly became obvious that she hadn't gotten the dead baby memo.

"So, it says here I need to take like six vials from you. Wow, that's a lot of blood," she whistled, looking at the order. "But I'm pretty good at this; it should go quick."

Goth Phlebotomist wrapped the rubber hose around my arm. "Make a fist. Good. Okay, small poke." I closed my eyes as the blood drained from me. "Almost done with the first vial... Okay, good, onto the next one...Shoot."

I opened my eyes. My vein had collapsed.

"All right, let's try this again. Wow, you have small veins." Another poke. "Gotcha! This one's going good...shoot!"

After three vials and eight veins, Julia poked her head in the door. "Everything okay in here?" I must have looked exasperated, for she was at my bedside at once. "Is there a problem?" she asked, staring accusingly at Goth Phlebotomist.

The young woman flinched, shifting her weight from one foot to the other. "Well, it was going fine, but now the veins are all collapsing, and it's getting a little harder. But I think I still got it."

She'd been drawing blood for at least thirty minutes, and I was quickly developing an arm that could have belonged to a junkie. Julia shot me an apologetic smile as she pulled on a pair of latex gloves. "Why don't I give it a try; I'm pretty good at taming wild veins."

Within five minutes Goth Phlebotomist was exiting my room with the requested six vials of blood.

"I'm sorry about that," the nurse apologized. "Sometimes the night shift doesn't exactly staff the best of the best."

I wanted to tell her that being treated like a pincushion didn't bother me since I was still numb with shock, but I didn't want to be dramatic.

"That's all right," I replied. "They always have a hard time drawing my blood." This was somewhat true; whenever I had a blood draw there was a fifty-fifty shot they would get it the first try.

"Do you two want to get some sleep, or can we talk a little more?"

Sleep? I had forgotten about that.

"Talk about what?" Chris asked, sitting up in his chair.

The nurse rolled her stool back up to the left side of the bed. "Well, we need to talk about the next steps."

It took me a minute to process her words. "You mean, getting it out?" I asked. It still made me feel better to think of Avery as an it rather than a person.

"Yes, that's what I mean."

From the second I'd been told of my daughter's death, I'd been desperate to hear "the solution," the simple answer to all of my problems that would make this hell go away once and for all. I wanted to be entirely selfish. I wanted to forget this night, to bury the past eight and a half months and stop thinking about Avery. I longed to travel back in time, to start all over with a different pregnancy and a different baby that would be born alive. There was an irrational part of me that actually believed it could happen, if only they would give me *the goddamn solution*.

Yet there was a larger, more logical part of me, the maternal part, that wasn't ready for my pregnancy to end. I loved that *thing* inside of me, that baby girl, more than I had ever loved anything before. I'd carried her with me everywhere, day and night, for what seemed an eternity. I was supposed to be a lioness, to fight for my cub, to do everything possible to save her from the clutches of death.

This was a pivotal moment—the moment that would change everything in my life. Once I gave birth to Avery, I would no longer be a pregnant woman; I would be a childless mother. These "next steps" meant admitting defeat, acknowledging that my daughter was really dead and there was nothing left to do but say goodbye.

How do you say goodbye to a child when you've never been given the chance to say hello?

"Okay," I whispered, fighting back tears. "What do we do next?"

Julia spent the next ten minutes explaining the induction

process. They would give me a drug, Cytotec, to ripen my cervix since my body hadn't begun labor on its own. The drug was supposed to "jump-start" my labor. The dose would be small, and they'd keep adding it as needed, as every woman reacted differently to the drug. It could take a few hours or it could take a few days; it all depended on what my body decided to do. After the Cytotec began working, I would receive an oxytocin IV to speed things up.

"Is this making sense?" Julia inquired, searching my blank stare. It was a lot of technical information to absorb, but I got the general idea.

"Yeah, I think so," I answered.

The nurse continued on with The Plan. Once I was fully dilated and my contractions were strong enough, we would begin pushing. It was going to more difficult than a standard labor, as I wouldn't be getting help from the baby. It was going to be hard, and it was going to be uncomfortable. The doctors would also pump me full of IV antibiotic, since keeping Avery inside of me for so long after my water broke put me at risk for infection and could make me septic. It was the first time I had even considered my own safety.

"Did you plan on getting an epidural?"she asked.

"Yes, definitely," I said. I had no illusions of being one of those superhuman moms that push through the pain.

"We can still do that," she said. "To be honest, it's probably a good idea. Do you have any other questions?"

Julia had been very thorough and very honest. I racked my brain for a minute and it came up blank. "No, I think we're good," I answered.

"Couldn't we just do a C-section?" Chris asked. "Wouldn't that be a lot easier?"

"Well, yes, it would be easier, but the risks are greater with a Cesarean, and Heidi's recovery would take a lot longer. With stillbirths, we like to do vaginal deliveries whenever possible, especially in women who will be having more children," Julia replied.

She paused for a moment, giving us room to ask more questions. Her pause was met with silence. How the hell did she know I'd be having more children? *I* wasn't even sure of that yet.

"Think about when you want to get started. We can do it whenever you're ready. But definitely take your time—we don't want to rush you. If you think of any questions, let me know." She leaned over and touched my arm as she stood up. "You two need to try and get some sleep. I'll be back in a few hours."

Stillbirths. It was the first time Julia had used that term with Avery. It was so technical, so clinical, so matter-of-fact.

I didn't like it.

I'd heard the term before, maybe in a magazine or on television, but never put any thought into it, because it was something that didn't pertain to me. Stillbirths were something that happened in third-world countries where poverty-stricken women delivered malnourished babies on dirt floors. Stillbirths were something that drug-using prostitutes had. Stillbirths were something other people had, people who lived in trailer parks with abusive boyfriends and didn't have healthcare.

Yet here I was, an educated, healthy, upper-middle-class high school teacher, the daughter of two doctors, having a stillbirth. I felt so dirty, so ashamed, like I had done something terribly wrong.

It was after five a.m., and the night sky was taking on the misty grayness of dawn. The stars had disappeared, and morning was officially breaking. Chris went to the window and slowly closed the blackout shades.

"I'm fucking tired," he said, climbing onto the vinyl pullout couch to the right of my bed. It was narrow, and his large frame looked hideously out of place on the clinical piece of furniture.

"Me too," I whispered, rolling onto my side. Our noses were inches apart; I could smell exhaustion in his stale breath.

"I don't know if I'm going to be able to sleep," he said.

"Me either."

We were both nauseated by fatigue yet terrified to let go and sleep. Closing our eyes was giving up, giving in to the wretched reality that our daughter was dead and we were completely helpless. No matter what we did, no matter what we said, Avery could not be saved. Yet if we stayed awake we at least felt like we were doing something, and somehow that made us feel a little less powerless.

Sleep was also dangerous. It would allow us to go somewhere else for a while, to momentarily forget our pain and have a brief respite from the Lifetime movie we were currently starring in.

And then we would wake up a few hours later, and we would have to remember all over again.

A part of me was certain if I just closed my eyes tight enough I'd wake up in my own big, cozy bed, miles away from the sterile loneliness of the hospital room. We'd all be safe and sound, this terrible nightmare behind us, Avery alive and kicking. I'd wake Chris and tell him about my awful dream; we'd make pancakes dripping with maple syrup and laugh about my silly pregnancy hormones.

We held each other tightly in silence, each listening to the other breathe in the darkness. It wasn't long before my exhausted husband's breaths became slower, deeper, rougher, a sure sign of sleep. I kissed him on the forehead and rolled onto my back.

Staring into the darkness, alone at last, I let the tears fall, hot and wet, soaking my tired face.

At some point I drifted off to sleep, only to be woken by the sound of soft weeping. I'm not sure who was crying: my husband, my daughter, or me.

CHAPTER SEVEN

My bladder woke me at seven a.m. As my feet hit the cold tile, Chris popped up from his makeshift bed and grabbed my wrist. "Is everything okay? Are you okay?"

"I'm fine, go back to sleep," I whispered, finding his concern sweet and amusing. "I just have to pee."

He slowly pulled his hand over his face, rubbing his eyes. I watched as the synapses began firing back memories in his head. He aged ten years right in front of me. "Are you still leaking?"

"No, not really. I think it's just about stopped," I glanced at my bed and the pads I had soiled in my hour of sleep. "It looks like it's all on the bed."

I went to the closet to get a new set of pads. "Here, give me those," my husband demanded, grabbing them from my hands. "I'll do that, you sit down."

I acquiesced, slumping down in a visitor's chair.

"It just doesn't seem real," he muttered sourly, making my bed.

"I know," I sighed.

"It's not fair. It's just not. How could this happen?" he choked, forcefully opening the shades and looking out the window at the sunny July day. "It makes me so…" I joined him at the window as he clenched his fists. "I need to call work."

My stomach sank as I contemplated what that meant. Avery's death would be announced, and other people would know. Up until that point I could easily have been trapped in a dream. Once word spread, everything would be real.

I watched restlessly as Chris dialed his Blackberry. I was tempted to grab the phone from his hands and smash it. I could vaguely hear his boss's voicemail.

"Hi, this is Chris. I wanted to let you know that I won't be in today… I'm at the hospital with Heidi. There was a problem… Avery didn't make it. Call me if you need anything."

And like that it was over. The secret was out.

"Are you going to call your parents?" Chris asked, offering me his phone.

I looked at the clock. It was Tuesday. My parents share a medical practice, and my dad had the day off and my mom was working. I couldn't just call and tell them their granddaughter was dead—not when my mom had patients to see.

"I'm going to wait until they get home from work," I decided. "What about you?"

Chris's parents were retired and lived in South Carolina. "I'll call them this afternoon."

We returned to our assigned positions, me in the bed, Chris next to me on the dreadful vinyl couch. Julia scooted in just as I tuned the TV to the *Today* show. Together we watched an ancient Willard Scott introduce his Smuckers geriatric lineup of the day. I found it ironic that some woman in Mississippi could live to be a hundred and six yet my daughter couldn't even live one day.

"Good morning, guys," she smiled softly, taking a seat on the stool. "Did you manage to get any sleep?"

"A little bit," I answered, nervous that she had come for my decision on starting labor.

"I just had to come in and see you guys. There's this other woman on the floor that just had a baby, and, well, let's just say she's a real piece of work." Julia scowled, rolling her eyes. "I had to get away from her and come talk to some normal people. It's just not fair. She has a nice, healthy baby and she's a complete bitch, and you guys are going through something so terrible, and you're so nice. I just wanted to tell you guys that that really shows your character. You're good people, and that makes this even sadder."

"Well, thanks," I said, touched by her honesty. Despite my misery, it was nice to know that at least I wasn't a bitch.

"Do you want us to go talk to her?" Chris joked tartly, flashing a devilish smile.

"No, no," Julia laughed. "You don't need to do that. But I had to stop myself from saying something to her about how lucky she is. Anyway, did you order breakfast yet?"

Breakfast? I hadn't even considered eating. "Not yet."

"The menu is right next to the phone. You both order whatever you'd like. They'll bring it up to you. Can I get you some water? Sprite?"

"Both?" I repeated. I was still dehydrated; my tongue felt like I had been licking sandpaper most of the night.

"Sure thing. I'll be back in a minute."

Julia reappeared with the liquids in less than sixty seconds, placing them on my bed's plastic dining tray. "My shift is over soon, but I'll be back before I go home. Get something to eat," she directed, pointing at the menu. "The food here isn't that bad."

We ordered breakfast and dined silently on an assortment of mediocre hospital pastries. It was a strange feeling, almost like we were on vacation at a one-star hotel. We hadn't had time to pack anything, so the entertainment was limited. We watched TV, stared at the walls, looked out the window, stared at each other. I caught myself rubbing my belly a few times, like I had when Avery was alive. Chris eventually started working and glued himself to his Blackberry, trying to find some way to pass the time.

My own concept of time was way off; minutes seemed like hours. I had a big decision to make, and it was eating away at my soul. The longer I waited, the longer I had a dead baby inside of me; the longer I waited, the more time I got to spend with my precious daughter. I wished someone would just make the call for me, but that wasn't possible. Or wise.

"I'm going to do it after I call my parents," I blurted out, turning to face Chris.

At first he looked confused. "Do what? Oh, the induction.

That's fine, we can do it whenever you want. You're the one who has to make the decision." He kissed my hand.

"Is that right?" I asked, looking for direction. My eyes begged for advice.

I knew exactly what he was going to say before he said it.

"It's up to you. You can do whatever you want."

We spent the rest of the day staring blankly at the TV and overanalyzing Avery's death. There had to be a logical reason for it, and we were determined to figure it out. We blamed our tragedy on too much time on the boat, on our trip to Mexico, on something I must have eaten. I had exercised too much; I didn't relax enough. I blamed the doctor I had seen three days prior, because he "should have known."

"I told him she wasn't moving as much," I pleaded to Chris. "He should have done something." But what I really felt was that I should have done something. Why didn't I demand a non-stress test or an ultrasound? Why did I trust that he knew best?

The more we examined our daughter's death, the angrier we became. The more we discussed her sudden demise, the more I blamed myself.

Never in my life had I felt like such a failure, so weak and so small. Hundreds of thousands of babies were born every day, all over the world. Babies were born in jungles, in barns, in huts; their mothers were somehow good enough to bring them into this world safely, yet I wasn't. I had failed at the one job that only I could do.

"I should have known," I found myself blubbering every five minutes. "How did I not know she was dying…how did I just let it happen…" I was stupid and useless, a disappointment as a mother, as a wife, and as a human being.

"It's not your fault," Chris assured me over and over. "There was nothing you could do." He tried to hold me, to console me, but I pulled away, ashamed for letting him down.

I didn't believe him, and I never would. I couldn't. I was certain that deep down people really believed Avery's death was my fault, even if it was just through my own ignorance. I was cloaked in shame, and I would forever wear the scarlet letter of the woman who allowed her helpless unborn baby to die.

We took a break from our Avery analysis to say goodbye to Julia, whose shift was finally up. She gave us both hugs and wished us the best.

Our new nurse wasn't as nice. She was older and didn't smile a lot; it was obvious she didn't want to be dealing with a wrecked young couple and their stillbirth. Her sullen demeanor was borderline rude, and I came close to telling her that I didn't want to be dealing with her, either.

Midafternoon, as I picked away at a surprisingly tasty hospital pizza, Chris picked up his phone.

I put a grease-laden slice down and glared at him, my pizza rising back up my throat. "What are you doing?" I growled.

"Calling my parents," he replied.

I wanted to tell him that he couldn't, that it wasn't fair if his parents knew and mine didn't. "Can't you wait?"

"They're far away. If they're going to drive up here, I need to let them know."

I didn't want them there. I didn't want anyone there except Chris. I had my own pain, my own shock; I didn't need to be surrounded by the grief of others. There just wasn't room in my brain to deal with my in-laws and their sorrow.

"What are you going to say?" I whispered as the lines connected.

Chris ignored me as his mother answered the phone. I angrily took another bite of pizza and listened to my husband tell his parents every detail of the last twelve hours. At times they were confused, no doubt in shock, and Chris would have to start all over again.

The once delicious pizza turned to cardboard in my mouth and my stomach churned. I put the food back on the plate, pushed it away, and rolled to my side, staring at the door.

Now more people knew, and it pissed me off for two reasons. The first was empathetic on my part: I didn't want to be the cause of such immense grief in our loved ones' lives. The second was more selfish: I didn't want people to blame me for what happened, and I was positive they would. Avery was inside of me when it happened. She was my responsibility, and I had failed her. I had failed everyone who loved her.

By the time my husband hung up the phone, his voice cracked and tears filled his eyes.

"They're going to fly up here," he said.

"Okay."

"Is that okay?"

"Yes."

"Are you sure?"

It wasn't okay, but I didn't really have a say. I turned to face him. "When?" I didn't want a room full of grandparents when I delivered their dead grandchild.

"Probably tomorrow."

"Okay."

Chris leaned over and gave me a kiss.

"Ewwww, you stink," he pulled back, waving a hand in front of his face.

"Whatever." I rolled my eyes. "So do you."

For the first time since I'd been admitted to the hospital, I took a good look at myself. I was a mess. My skin was clammy and greasy, my gown was soiled with dark stains, and I was pretty sure a flock of birds had taken up residence in my ratty hair. "I'm pretty gross, aren't I?" I admitted. No wonder the new nurse was so mean.

We paged the nurse, who brought the basic supplies I hadn't had the presence of mind to pack in the chaos of the previous night.

I stood up and pranced toward the bathroom (as much as I could prance, anyway.) "I'm taking a shower," I announced, closing the door.

"Thank God," I heard Chris joke as I started the water.

The shower was a temporary reprieve. It didn't improve the situation, but it made me feel more human. While the water didn't wash away the shock, pain, and confusion I was facing, it did rid me of the blood, and at least made me smell better. I dried off slowly with a tiny white hospital towel and made a half-hearted attempt to fix my frizzy blond hair. The pregnancy hormones made my hair twice as thick, and I wasn't used to having to tame my tresses. My feeble attempt at beauty seemed extraordinarily vain given the situation, but how does the saying go? When you look good, you feel good. And I was looking for any possible way to feel a little less terrible.

I walked out of the room and found Chris gazing out the window, lost in deep thought. I joined him, surveying the lives going on outside my hospital room.

It was a perfect July day in Michigan, a cloudless azure sky arcing over the green landscape. Even through the glass I could tell there was a slight breeze; it would have been a perfect day to be on our boat. I felt like Mother Nature was mocking our misery by giving us such beautiful weather on such a sad day. I wanted it to be gray and dreary, a day that screamed death. I wanted the skies to cry along with us.

"You gotta be fucking kidding me," Chris breathed, pointing.

We had a large window encompassing the entire north side of our room, which provided a spectacular view of a large parking lot. A woman no older than twenty was walking to her car, a fairly new baby in her arms and a messy toddler in tow. She placed the baby on the pavement as she lit a cigarette, swiftly swooping down to scoop the little one back up and blowing a big cloud of smoke in her tiny face. The toddler ran ahead, narrowly escaping a reversing car.

"How is it that people like that get to have kids and we don't?" He snorted. "It makes me sick."

I sighed, putting my arm around his slumped shoulders. "I don't know. I really don't," I tried. "But we get to have kids, too. Someday, we will…just not now. Just not Avery." I was surprised by my sudden enlightenment.

"But I want Avery."

"Me too."

"It's not fair."

"I know."

At 5:30 I finally called my parents. It was one of the most difficult things I'd ever done. My hands shook as I dialed the phone, and I fought the urge to hang up.

"Hello?" my mother's perky voice greeted me.

"Hi, Mom." My words were a little too long, a little too heavy.

There was a brief pause on the other end. She could tell something was wrong. "What's up?" A pang shot through my heart as I sensed her concern.

The words were hard to get out. "I have some bad news," I began, tears pooling. "It's Avery. We lost her."

My words were met with pained silence; then, "Oh, Heidi, I'm sorry. What happened?"

I hastily rehashed the details of our ordeal, at least what I could put together through the tears.

"Do you want me to come down there?" my mother asked. (My parents lived four hours away.)

"Yes," I whispered. My husband was wonderful, but I suddenly realized I needed my mommy.

"I'll work it out. I'll drive down tomorrow," she said. "I love you."

The news was spreading like a pandemic; I felt trapped in a twisted game of Telephone. For every one person we told, another twenty were notified, and then another twenty after that. All afternoon Chris received sympathy texts, emails, and phone calls from coworkers. Within an hour of talking to my mom, family started to call. I sent the majority of calls to voicemail; the only person I actually talked to was my older brother, also a doctor.

"God, I'm so sorry," he said. "I'm so sorry."

"Thanks," I said. What else was there to say?

"Not that it makes you feel any better, but when I was doing my OB rotation there was always someone like you on the ward, at least one," he said. "They never let us go in, since we were just students, but there was always one."

For some reason that did make me feel better. Being the

pariah of the maternity ward was lonely. It helped to know I wasn't entirely alone in the world, to know that this had happened to someone else, or might even be happening to someone else at that very moment. I had a sister out there somewhere, someone who truly knew my pain.

As the sun began to set, the nurse reappeared. She'd made herself scarce for the majority of the day.

"How are you doing in here?" she asked, all business.

"Good," I replied. I always said good when they asked, which we all knew was a lie. But what was I supposed to say—terrible? It was obvious that I was feeling terrible; I didn't need to say it. I looked hard at my husband, then back at the nurse. "I think I'm ready to, you know, start the process."

The nurse hastily grabbed a stool and sat down next to my bed. I noticed a manila folder tucked in her hands. "Okay," she said, half-smiling for the first time since I met her. "We can do that. I'll get the pills ready." The smile quickly disappeared as she pulled a paper from the folder. Her voice became softer. "We need to talk about disposal of the body."

I stared, wide-eyed, my mouth gaping in disbelief.

I was responsible for disposing of Avery?

"What do you mean?" I stuttered, confused. I looked at my husband; he was as dumbfounded as I was.

"Well, some parents choose to have a burial service for their child," she explained.

I almost laughed as I imagined inviting people to my baby's funeral. Would I send out invitations, like a birthday party? Maybe put together an Evite? Who would be the lucky invitees? Surely people would be clamoring to attend. The sour taste of bile burned my throat as I pictured the tiny casket holding my daughter's body.

"I don't think we want to do that," Chris answered, turning to me. "Do we?"

"No, no. We don't want that." I shook my head adamantly.

The nurse shook her head too, mirroring me as if in understanding. "Okay. The other option is cremation."

I wanted to ask if there was a third option. Perhaps making my daughter not be dead? I was tempted to ask why I couldn't just take her home and put her in her crib, but I didn't think this nurse would appreciate my sarcasm.

"We work with a funeral home, and they'll come and pick up the body." She spoke so softly I could barely hear her. I wondered if that was part of the sensitivity training she'd had in nursing school. "The funeral home will call you with more information, and they'll let you know when you can pick up the remains."

It was eerie, thinking of having my unborn daughter's remains in our house. But it was the best option, or at least the only option that made sense.

The nurse scribbled something on my chart, left the room, and quickly returned with my first dose of Cytotec. Chris and I settled in for a night of frustration and waiting. No one knew how my body would react to the drugs; I didn't know if I would be pushing in an hour or pushing in a week.

"How do you feel?" Chris asked.

"The same."

"Nothing?"

"Nope."

I looked at my husband, the man I had been with for most of my adult life. He looked so tired, so crushed. Bags hung low beneath his hazel eyes, and his tan face had taken on an unnatural shade of gray. He had aged so much in the past twenty-four hours. I wondered if people would say the same about me.

We once again stretched out on our respective beds and watched TV in silence. Hours ticked away like a molasses drip; the nurse returned.

"Are you feeling any change?"

"Nothing," I answered.

"I'll give you another dose." She handed me another pill. She twisted her mouth into a pursed smile. "It might help if you get up and move around the room, too. That can help move things along."

I watched as she left the room. "Did she just call me lazy?"

"I think so." Chris smiled, a bit of his boyish charm shining through his exhaustion. "Well, you heard the woman—get up and move."

I spent the next two hours attempting to move my fat, swollen body around the room. I walked laps. I did squats. We danced and jumped and flailed about the room, acting silly. I found myself laughing as Chris twirled me into a chair; I felt instant guilt at letting myself laugh. I moved as much as I could, but nothing changed. Not a cramp, not a pang, not an instinct to push. All was quiet in my womb.

The nurse popped her head in. "Anything?"

"Nope."

She handed me another pill, forcing a pained smile. "I'm off in a few minutes. I'll update the new nurse on your status."

"Thank you," I said dryly. I prayed the next nurse had a personality.

Nurse number three arrived within minutes. I don't remember much about her, other than that she was a lot nicer.

"It's getting pretty late," she said. "Would you like me to get you an Ambien? Sometimes the deep sleep really helps move things along."

The thought of a numbing, drug-induced slumber was tantalizing, but I hesitated to say yes. I didn't even like taking Advil when I had a headache. A forbidden fruit was being dangled in front of my face, and I was afraid of what would happen to me if I ate that tainted apple.

"I guess we could try that," I whispered, uncertainty lacing my words.

The nurse refilled my water and handed me a pill. "Get some sleep," she said. She turned and pointed at Chris. "You let me know if anything changes."

I took one last sip of water and gave my husband a kiss. I rested my weary head on the cardboard hospital pillow and closed my eyes. Within a minute my world collapsed into sweet darkness.

*****

Ancient superstitions link birds to the spirit world. Great misfortune is said to be tied to the death of one of our feathered friends, and since Roman times the death of a bird near a person's home has signified the upcoming death of a family member.

When I was seven and a half months pregnant with Avery, while traveling to one of my many baby showers a hundred miles away, two birds flew in front of our SUV. The first narrowly escaped the windshield; the second wasn't so lucky. I cringed as I heard the thud and saw the feathers fly. I looked out the rear window and watched the first bird, the survivor, waiting on the side of the highway for his companion, lost and confused.

Two weeks later, I heard the squawking of angry birds in our back yard. Thinking a squirrel was trying to dine on the robin's nest that had become a fixture on our back porch, I headed outside to shoo it away. I found no pesky rodents in the vicinity, but a dead robin lay motionless in the grass. Five other songbirds kept their distance in the nearby trees, chirping a funeral march for their fallen comrade. I donned a pair of gloves and disposed of the body.

Not even a week later, I opened the front door to walk to the mailbox. A tiny, motionless sparrow sat dead center on my front stoop. I originally blamed my cats for the carcass, but the placement of the body was odd for a cat, way too precise.

I couldn't get that poor little bird out of my head.

Less than two weeks later, I found out Avery was dead.

I wonder if someone was trying to tell me something.

*****

"Ohhhhh, ohhh. Uggg, ahhh…oh shit…"

I awoke to a black room and the sound of groaning. For a second I thought Chris was talking in his sleep, but as my eyes adjusted I realized he was awake and staring at me, concern filling the lines of his face.

A sharp lower back pain rendered me immobile.

"Ohhhh my God, holy crap, shit…"

I was the one making the noise.

"It's okay, it's okay," Chris tried to console me. "Where does it hurt?"

"Oh God, everywhere, oh shit…" I moaned miserably as an invisible knife stabbed my spine and twisted.

"Should I call the nurse?"

"What time is it?"

"Three."

"No, I think I'm…oh God…"

I'd never experienced such unnatural pain in my life, as if my midsection was being pierced repeatedly with shards of jagged glass. My abdomen quivered and burned with a pain so intense it consumed every inch of flesh in its fiery grasp. My back twisted and pulsed. The blood in my veins coursed thicker and thicker, until it pooled in my head, throbbing in tandem with the rest of the torture. For the first time in my life I thought I could truly die. Before I could focus on my surroundings again, the nurse was at my side.

"Well, it looks like something's happening," she clucked.

I wanted to slap her.

As the next wave of pain and nausea devoured me, she checked my dilation and frowned. "You're still only at one."

"You're kidding me," I grunted, curling into the fetal position, weeping helplessly.

Chris stood at my side, stroking my sweat-drenched hair. "Can we do something for the pain?"

"I can give you a painkiller if you'd like."

"Oh, yes, please," I groaned.

The next round of pills came, followed by another round of darkness.

The rest of the night was blurry, like watching television in a funhouse mirror. I drifted in and out of consciousness. I'd wake in a pool of sweat, screaming in agony, clawing at the dark for support. I'd latch onto a terrified Chris, restlessly sitting at my bedside ready to attend to my every need, and promptly lose consciousness.

The painkillers numbed the pain but didn't stop it. I'd sleep briefly and wake whenever a contraction hit. It was very psychedelic, like a cracked-out version of *Sesame Street*, but every time I felt a contraction come on I would see a letter of the alphabet, glowing neon green against a black curtain. As the contraction strengthened, the letter would get bigger; as the contraction ceased, the letter shrank, finally disappearing into the shadows. I'd never done acid, but I was fairly certain I was tripping.

I don't remember this, but at some point in the night I got up to use the bathroom. Evidently I spent a great deal of time in there; Chris began to worry. I met my husband outside the doorway, stumbled, and warned him to "Watch out for the trees." I crawled back in bed and passed out.

Before I could blink, my drug-induced haze was over and the room filled with sunshine. There were people in my room, and I was hit with complete lucidity. I was in an inordinate amount of pain, yet the clarity was remarkable. Colors were brighter, sounds were louder, voices were crisper.

My doctor walked in, his scrubs gloriously blue. He spoke briefly to the nurse and sat down next to me. As I winced in pain, he explained that I was dilating slowly but they thought I might be getting close. He went on about how they were going to monitor and *blah blahblahblahblah*. I couldn't hear him over my latest contraction.

"Can I have an epidural now?" I asked, gritting my teeth.

"Yes, we'll get the anesthesiologist in here for you," he answered.

Within minutes an attractive young doctor sauntered in, spoke to the nurse, and stuck a massive needle in my back. My pain drifted away like a party balloon.

As my legs turned to bricks, the nurse inserted a catheter in my urethra, and for the first time in my life I was truly immobile.

"You feel better?"Chris asked.

"Oh my God, I feel so much better," I answered, smiling, my face able to convey a feeling other than pain for the first time in hours.

Two nurses quietly worked on me, prepping me for delivery. They hooked up a monitor to my belly to measure the strength of my contractions. We had all hoped the screen would show it was time to start pushing, but the contractions were disappointingly weak.

I lay in the hospital bed, my temporary home, a handful of drugs and other fluids dripping into an IV in my arm, the liquid processed by my stationary body draining into a bag hooked to the side of the bed. We watched the monitor as a large contraction hit.

"You don't feel that?"the older nurse asked.

"Nope," I answered.

"Good."

My contractions were all over the place in strength, which meant it would be pointless to start pushing. Chris and I sat and waited, something we were becoming very good at, our eyes flicking back and forth from the *Today* show to the contraction monitor.

Around ten in the morning there was a knock on the door. A nurse's head poked through the crack.

"You have a visitor. Is that okay?" she asked as a short older woman shoved the nurse aside, determined to enter the room.

"Mom," I sighed.

Her eyes welled with tears as she sat down on the edge of my bed. She smiled and gave me a long hug, hesitating to let go.

My mother listened quietly and I relayed the specifics of my story, trying to hold back my tears like a grown-up. I did my best to be strong, to stifle my emotions, because that's how my family typically operated. Yet something about having my mother there made me feel like a child again, which made crying seem a little more okay.

"It's going to be all right," my mom said, holding my hand. "Everything's going to be all right."

My mother is an amazingly strong woman, but I could tell that seeing me broke her heart. I knew she wasn't just saying everything would be all right for my sake; she was also saying it to herself.

An hour went by and my contractions refused to cooperate. A nurse returned to give us an update.

"I think we're going to try to start pushing soon," she said. "Your contractions aren't ideal, but you're getting a few good waves. The doctor thinks we should try to use those while we can, before they go away completely and we have to reassess."

After almost nine months, the moment I had agonized over had finally arrived. I was terrified of giving birth long before I got pregnant, scared of the pain and worried that I just couldn't do it. It was now time to face my fears, for my darling Avery was finally going to leave my womb and enter the world. But I'd never imagined my first child would come into the world like this.

The nurse took a seat and began to get very specific about what was going to happen after Avery came out. I was startled, because my brain was focused solely on the process of getting her out. I hadn't considered the aftermath.

"Typically we rest the baby on the mother's stomach," she said. "Would you like to do that?"

"No, no, no." I shook my head violently. The thought of Avery's lifeless body resting on me was too much.

"Okay, I understand. If you'd like we can take her and clean her off, get her dressed," she continued. "And then would you like to hold her?"

I tried over and over to wrap my brain around her words. Did I want to hold my dead daughter? No, I wanted to hold my living daughter. That wasn't an option. But did I really want to see her? What if she looked scary, like something from a horror movie? I didn't want to see Avery that way. But I also didn't want to go through the rest of my life regretting not seeing her.

"Do I have to tell you now?" I whispered, closing my eyes against the indecision.

"No, you can decide later." She smiled, touching my shoulder. "Just so you're aware, if you do decide to look at her, she will most likely be pale with rosy cheeks. She may have a white film on her. That's just vernix—that's normal on babies. Her skin may be peeling a little. Her lips will most likely be purple."

"Thanks," I breathed, suddenly convinced my baby would look like a monster. I didn't want to see her. But did I *need* to?

"And then we also like to take pictures, so we'll do that as well, if you'd like."

I stared at the nurse, unblinking. I couldn't believe what I was hearing. They were going to take pictures of my dead child? Were they insane? Smile and say cheese! You just delivered a dead baby. What a joyous occasion. Let's take a family shot!

The nurse read my mind through the look on my face. "You don't have to look at them, you can just lock them away, but I think you'll find that down the road you'll be happy you have them."

"Okay" was all I could muster. I was overwhelmed; I wanted to run far away, away from this terrible dream and all of these crazy people who were trying to "help" me. I wanted to float to an alternate universe where my life wasn't in shambles.

The nurse looked at Chris. "Would you like to hold her?"

"Yes, of course," he said bluntly. I was jealous of his confidence.

"I'll be back in a few minutes, and we'll get things started."

My mom looked at me with a weary smile. "Do you want me to stay in the room?"

She was a pediatrician and had witnessed thousands of deliveries, both happy and sad. But I couldn't let her see this. This was my moment of pure hell, and I didn't want her to watch me suffer.

"No, I don't think so."

She kissed me on the forehead and started to leave the room, turning back at the door. "I'm proud of you. You're being so strong," she said, flashing one last teary smile. "Have them come get me as soon as it's over."

Chris and I were alone for less than a minute before the delivery team entered the room.

"Here we go," I breathed, praying it went quickly. "Here we go."

CHAPTER EIGHT

The birth of my daughter was terrible for everyone involved. First off, no one was excited to deliver a dead baby. On top of that, my contractions were far from ideal. I would have one large contraction followed by long, tedious stretches of calm.

It was a strange scene, almost comical in its own absurd way. I had a heavy-duty epidural, so I felt nothing below my waist. Movement was impossible; my deadened legs dangled like wet noodles from my torso. I wasn't even sure if I still had legs. A delivery nurse was stationed on my left and Chris stood on my right. This leg-holding team held my knees firmly in the air, keeping me in the proper pushing position, always on guard for a usable contraction. The doctor sat patiently between my open legs, staring at my lady parts, apprising us of any progress.

During the long contraction-less stretches we stayed in our designated positions and alternated between awkward silence and small talk.

We chatted about how I'd played soccer in high school and how I liked to run before I got pregnant. Chris spoke of his job and how he'd like to move to a warmer climate. I spent a good thirty minutes explaining what it was like teaching high school journalism. I felt like I was at a cocktail party and we should all be wearing nametags. In reality, I was going through the most traumatic experience of my life.

The worst part of the delivery wasn't the pain or the pushing or the chitchat or displaying my vagina for virtual strangers for three hours. The worst part was the glimmer of hope that I foolishly held onto, the tiny voice in my head that kept whispering that miracles do happen, and that maybe, just maybe, it was all a big misunderstanding. My baby girl would come out squealing and pissed off like every other baby, and the doctor would say, "Whoops! Now that was a big mistake." Chris and I would be so overcome with joy and love for our daughter that we'd instantly forgive his error, and we'd laugh and hug and exchange high fives.

He didn't have to say it, but I could tell from my husband's anxious face that he was thinking the same thing.

After two slow, grueling hours of pushing, Avery's head finally made it to the birth canal. Since she wasn't giving us any help, it took a great deal of effort and even more Astroglide to coax her farther.

"It's the cord," I heard the doctor sigh, reaching for a pair of surgical scissors. He nodded at Chris. "Did you want to cut the cord?"

I was confused; Avery's shoulders weren't even out yet, but they were cutting the cord?

There was some commotion between my legs as Chris received instructions. In a minute he returned to my side, his face somber and drained. He explained how tight the cord was, wrapped around her tiny neck twice. They had to cut it just to pull the rest of my daughter's body out.

I looked back up at Chris. Any illusion he had of miracles had been extinguished with that tiny snip.

"Just a few more pushes. Good, good…"

The last minutes of the delivery felt like they happened in slow motion, an eternity passing in a heartbeat. I grunted and gave one last thrust, and the mild pressure that lingered in my pelvis subsided.

At 1:43 p.m. on a beautiful July afternoon, my sweet Avery's body came into this world.

I closed my bloodshot eyes and held my breath, praying, waiting for the sweet sound that would tell me it was all an enormous mistake.

I made a deal with God, and I waited.
And waited.
But there was no miracle that day.
Only the terrible sound of silence.

*****

I've always been a cat person. I believe that animals have a sixth sense—they know more than us simple humans and have a strange connection to the unseen and the unknown. I grew up with a cat, Kitty, who was there to play with me during my happy childhood, to love me during that awkward prepubescent phase, and to cuddle and listen to me cry over the earth-shattering drama of high school. She was a fierce feline, roaming the woods and picking fights with raccoons, but during her twenty-one years of life she always knew when I needed her. It was only natural that as an adult I acquired two cats of my own.

When I was six months pregnant with Avery, a friend gave me a shopping bag filled with baby towels. It was a sturdy brown paper bag with rope handles; I set the bag on a rocking chair in Avery's bedroom, too tired to put them away.

That night I awoke at two a.m., my heart racing, certain I heard strange noises from upstairs. I sat still in the darkness, trying to discern what had roused me. All I could hear was my own breath, mixed with my husband's slumberous respiration. As I tried to fall back to sleep, I heard a soft thumping noise, followed by an eerie rustling. The cats, I thought angrily. The troublemaker, Lulu, had no doubt gotten into something, but I was too tired and annoyed to care. It could wait until morning.

After five minutes, the noises grew louder. I reluctantly dragged myself out of bed to put an end to her nocturnal fun. I walked to the living room, flipped the light, and found the entire length of the stairs blanketed in baby towels. The trail continued into Avery's nursery.

The towels were accounted for, but I was still missing the bag and the cats.

I searched the upstairs rooms and found Nina, the older cat of the two, sleeping peacefully on a spare bed. She yawned irritably as I turned on the light, quickly covering her eyes with a paw. She was not the culprit.

Back downstairs in the living room, I was greeted with nothing but silence. "Lulu?" I whispered, growing tired of her games. "Lulu, where the hell are you?"

I was seconds away from returning to bed when I heard an eerie sound in the dining room, a small wheeze followed by the crackle of a bag. As I neared the table, the wheezing grew more frantic, the crackling more reckless.

"What the…" I got down on my knees.

I found Lulu wedged under a chair, her tiny pink tongue hanging from her mouth, green eyes bulging, desperately gasping for air. The brown bag floated against the bottom of the chair, the rope handle wrapped tightly around my cat's neck twice. She stared at me helplessly, her eyes begging, moments away from her last breath.

"Oh my God," I gasped, adrenaline taking over as I stumbled to the kitchen for scissors. "It's going to be okay, Lulu. Just hang in there."

With shaking hands, I tried to pry the rope from Lulu's neck, hoping to get enough slack to safely make a cut, but the rope was unbelievably tight and wouldn't yield. The cat's body was tense but still, and I said a prayer as I wedged the scissors against her neck and clamped down on the twine. The pressure instantly released. As I unwrapped the rope from her neck, Lulu slumped to the floor, gasping for air. Unsure of what to do next, I sat with the cat for an hour, hoping she wouldn't die.

Two months after Avery was born, Lulu walked out our back door, never to be seen again.

*****

I tried not to look as the doctor pulled Avery's limp body from me, but my eyes wouldn't listen to my brain. I had waited nine months—hell, thirty-two years—to see my baby girl. And there she was, right in front of me.

Slimy and purple and still.

"The cord was pretty tight around her neck," the doctor began. "We'll do an autopsy, run other tests…"

"How did that happen?" Chris asked quietly.

The doctor explained that it was fairly common, that about twenty-five percent of babies are born with a cord around their neck. But most of those cords are wrapped loosely and don't result in death. Avery's vise was a minority statistic.

I was tired of hearing statistics.

Once the cord was cut from Avery's belly and she was free of the noose my own body had created, the older nurse silently took her to the sink to be washed and dressed.

I watched the ritual curiously from my bed while the doctor stitched me up, wondering what my little girl looked like. Chris, who hadn't let go of my hand in hours, leaned over me and showered my face with kisses. "You did great," he smiled. "You did." I had never seen him look at me that way, with such admiration and respect.

"Thanks," I sighed, squeezing his hand. I was worn out mentally and physically, yet I couldn't help feeling a sense of accomplishment, that rush of euphoria and hormones that new mothers have. But my hard work was for nothing.

I watched as the nurse worked, as the doctor finished his notes, as Chris, who had been standing the entire morning, finally settled into his bedside chair. The room was so quiet, quiet in the way that makes a person long to cut off their ears so they no longer have to listen to the absence of noise. It was a nauseating silence, the kind that accompanies death.

I lay in the bed, exhausted, envisioning how it would feel to have that quiet broken by the sweet wail of a newborn baby.

I silently vowed to be back in that bed in a year, listening to my second child cry.

CHAPTER NINE

Death is a strange thing for the living. It's a mystery, an enigma wrapped in a miserable riddle, yet it inevitably touches us all. It evokes confusion, fear, anguish, relief.

The first time I saw a dead body I was a wide-eyed seven-year-old reluctantly attending my maternal grandfather's funeral. Like most children, I didn't fully grasp the concept of death, and as I stood over his casket I expected to see something, to feel something, but it was simply the body of a graying man in his sixties, seemingly ancient in the ignorance of my youth. I touched his face and shuddered at the chill of his skin. I waited for his eyes to open one last time, for him to sit up and hug me and say one last goodbye. But nothing happened. I walked away.

Death had graciously touched me only a handful of times—never anything monumental, simply the expected passing of aging family members who had lived full, happy lives.

And then came Avery.

My mom was the first family member to see her. As the nurse finished bathing my daughter on the other side of the room, my mother snuck in unnoticed and peeked over the woman's shoulder.

"She's beautiful," the teary nurse whispered, smiling.

My mom stroked Avery's face, a proud grandmother. "She really is," she cooed.

The two women chatted while Avery was carefully dressed, and I watched silently as the woman responsible for my existence held her only granddaughter tightly in her arms. She stared longingly at her for a few minutes and then walked to my bed.

"Would you like to hold her?" she asked, offering me my daughter.

I looked at the wall and wiped my tears. "Sure," I exhaled, doing my best to sit up. My epidural was still going strong.

My mom carefully placed Avery in my shaking arms and let go. Her body, still warm, was surprisingly heavy.

"She's so big," I breathed, amazed by the weight. "I didn't think she'd be so big."

"Six pounds, fourteen ounces," the nurse chimed in from across the room. "Nineteen and a half inches. A perfect size."

She was swaddled tightly in a pink-and-blue-striped hospital blanket. A pink knit hat graced her dainty head, covering a mess of black curls.

I stared at her in silence, desperately trying to burn the moment into my mind, snapping a mental picture I could look at over and over. I had a very short time to be with my daughter face to face, and I wanted to remember, needed to remember, every dark curl on her head and blemish on her face, to remember every ounce of flesh and how it felt in my arms.

Someone spoke, but I ignored the words and refused to look away from my daughter's face, the sweetest face I'd ever laid eyes on. She had the chubbiest cheeks—a cherub straight from an Italian Renaissance painting. Her jowls were perfect for pinching, and I'm certain she would have spent her holidays hiding from the eager fingers of the geriatric crowd.

Her eyes, though closed in eternal slumber, were large and almond-shaped like her father's, and I was certain they were brown beneath the pale lids. Her parted lips were pouty red bows, and I couldn't help but think of all the strawberries I'd eaten. I pressed my fingers to the crimson flesh, foolishly expecting to feel her warm breath on my hand.

"She really is beautiful," I sighed through my tears.

Her only imperfection was a bruise across her forehead, the discoloration caused by her head repeatedly banging against my pelvis as she hung from her noose. I shuddered as I ran my fingers across the mark.

From the moment I learned of her death, I had been petrified she would be hideous, that I would be bringing a disfigured monster into this world. She was not the revolting sight I feared, but a precious little baby, a sleeping newborn full of sugar and innocence.

She was a beautiful baby. A sweet, beautiful, sleeping baby.

It made me feel good that I had created something so perfect.

It made me feel terrible that I had lost something so perfect.

I pressed my forehead to hers and inhaled her newborn smell; she smelled fresh and earthy, like soil after a rainstorm. I never wanted to forget that smell.

I stared at Avery for thirty minutes, waiting for her to open her eyes and yawn, for her tiny mouth to start rooting for food, for her tiny hands to reach out to me for comfort. In an instant the sensation of satisfaction subsided and panic consumed me. I couldn't hold her anymore; I couldn't look at her. I almost threw her at my husband like a football.

"Your turn," I sniffed, fighting my emotions.

Watching Chris hold our daughter was the final blow. My soul quivered as he touched her hair and stroked her face. I was seconds from losing control when I noticed the nurse standing at my bedside, holding my hand. She looked at me and smiled, the lines on her tired face creasing.

"If I hadn't lost my first child, I wouldn't have my son today," she said, patting my hand. "And I love my son more than anything."

Her words echoed in my head as she exited the room. For a split second I felt a spark in my heart; it was quickly extinguished by darkness. Yet I couldn't help but reflect on her words and see a glimmer of hope for our future. She had lost a child, and she had survived. Because of her pain, she now had someone she loved more than anything. Someday I might have someone I loved more than anything because of my pain—because of Avery's pain.

My in-laws arrived, and the large room began to shrink. More somber hugs were exchanged; more tears fell. A nurse came in to take pictures. We took turns holding Avery and smiling awkwardly for the camera. The grandmothers sat in the rocking chair and took turns rocking the baby. I found their behavior pathetic and creepy and spent the most of the time staring blindly at the wall. The pictures from that day are purely heartbreaking. The grandparents look so proud; the parents look so defeated.

The photographer told us we could keep Avery with us as long as we wanted, then disappeared to give us privacy.

I eventually had the desire to hold my baby again, partly because I was tired of everyone else holding her, but mostly because I feared I was already forgetting her face.

She was still warm when she returned to my arms. The first time I held her I was afraid to unwrap the blanket and see the rest of her body. Now, with all of the handling, her blanket had come unwrapped, and she was finally exposed.

Her hands were lily white, drenched in the purest snow, with tiny, trimmed pink fingernails. She had her father's hands, short fingers and big palms. I wrapped her little fingers in my own and thought how that sweet hand would never play patty-cake or skip a stone. I would never hold that hand as we crossed the street or teach those fingers how to play piano. That hand would never throw a ball or wave bye-bye or wear an engagement ring. I opened up her fingers and sighed, stroking her palm, hoping she could feel the love in my touch.

From the moment Avery arrived, my hospital room was filled with people. But I longed to be alone, allowed to bond with my daughter privately. Watching everyone else's misery was pissing me off; I was the one who'd carried her inside of me for nine months. I was the one who gave birth to her. I was the one who'd let her die. Everyone else needed to leave and let me deal with that.

Finally, around three p.m., the grandparents left to get lunch. Chris, who hadn't left my side in three days, went home to shower, change, and pack me a suitcase.

I finally got the chance to be alone with my daughter.

Avery rested in her hospital bassinet near my bed, silent and sleeping, the perfect baby. I rolled onto my side and stared at her, amazed at her perfection and equally devastated by her silence.

As I gazed longingly at my baby girl, a surprise storm rolled in, blanketing the sunny day in darkness. Lightning cut the gray sky in half, and I felt the electricity in my fingertips. Angry rain pounded the hospital windows, flooding the streets outside. The power flashed on and off, on and off, finally sending the hospital onto generator power. It was like a scene from Frankenstein. I stared at Avery, waiting for lightning to slice through the window and strike the bassinet, miraculously bringing my child back to life. I'd have my own Baby Frankenstein, but she would be alive. When the storm passed, I was still empty-handed. No unholy events occurred other than massive flooding and power outages, and those didn't really matter to me, at least not then.

I listened to the thunder and considered how out of place the storm was on that beautiful day, like a bulging red pimple on the face of the Mona Lisa. Yet it was fitting for a day where everything was sideways. The storm came out of nowhere, surprising drivers and meteorologists alike, demolishing a perfect day—just as death had blindsided my perfect family and destroyed my perfect child. I decided it was Avery's final way of saying goodbye, and she was determined to make sure I got the message.

I spent over an hour staring at my daughter, self-loathing boiling in my veins. Solitude gave me time to reflect, which I needed, but I couldn't stop myself from scrutinizing every single step of my pregnancy over and over. She had died inside of me, so it had to be something I did. No one else could be the scapegoat. I was group B positive—was there a leak I didn't notice? I should have demanded antibiotics for my entire pregnancy. It could have been the fish I ate, the Diet Coke I drank, the feta cheese. What was I thinking, going to Mexico for a vacation?

I was so stupid.

I should have stayed off the boat. I shouldn't have used the elliptical machine or run in the first trimester. Avery and I snowshoed all winter; maybe that was too much exertion. I shouldn't have planted flowers that spring. I lifted too many heavy things. I should have rested more, eaten more, slept more, counted more...

I should have done more.

Stupid, stupid, stupid.

How could I have not realized something was wrong with my child? How did I not know her heart had stopped? I was a terrible mother, a terrible person. I didn't deserve to have children. I had failed Avery because I was too stupid and too selfish to notice anything was wrong.

I tried to trace back every second of that last week to determine the moment Avery's heart beat for the last time. I thought of her last moments. There was a day I felt her foot wedged up in my rib. Was she trying to tell me something? Was she asking for help? I needed to know when she died and what I was doing when it happened. Was I sleeping? Eating? Walking? Watching TV? I imagined her flailing around in my womb, desperately trying to free her neck from the cord, wondering why Mommy wasn't helping her. She must have felt so scared and alone.

Knowing would give me the closure I needed. But it was impossible to know.

I thought of God, the all-powerful being I was supposed to look to for guidance, and I began to hate Him. I was a good person, a nice person, a righteous person. What had I done to deserve such pain? I was certain I was being punished, that in my hesitation to become a mother I somehow didn't want Avery enough, that I didn't love her enough, so He took her away from me to teach me a lesson.

God was spiteful and immature, and I was through with Him until He apologized.

I was quickly brought out of my head as the cavalry returned, first my mother, then the in-laws. Chris, the only person I really wanted to see, arrived later than expected due to the downed trees and power lines triggered by Avery's farewell storm.

A nurse returned to unhook my catheter and get me on my feet. "Do you think you can stand?" she asked, helping me scoot to the edge of the bed.

That was a silly question, I thought, getting to my feet. The effects of the epidural were gone, and I was confident my legs were back to normal. But as my feet met the cold tile my legs felt oddly unsteady. The more weight I put on them, the more they shook.

"Okay, slowly now," the nurse directed, holding my right arm. I took a small step forward and immediately collapsed to the floor, my legs buckling under me like a newborn colt. I heard my mother-in-law gasp as I kissed the tile.

I laughed nervously, looking at the nurse for reassurance, hoping she'd tell me what I was experiencing was normal.

She looked worried.

"Was that supposed to happen?" I chuckled, trying to be positive.

She paused, choosing her words carefully. "Well, no, that's not typical. But it's different for everyone. We can try again later."

I can be obstinate, and trying again later wasn't going to cut it. I refused to be shackled to that hospital bed, and I was ready to get back to "normal" as soon as possible. "No," I said. "I can do it." Besides, my catheter had been removed. What if I needed to pee?

The nurse acquiesced and took my arm. Chris grabbed my other side and I struggled to the bathroom, nearly falling three times during the ten-foot trip.

Once on the toilet, I was pleased that I was still able to urinate, since walking was such an issue. At least one body part was working. When I tried to get off the toilet, however, I found I needed help. I was glad Chris had insisted on staying in the room with me.

"I can't do it," I moaned weakly, feeling like a toddler. "I can't get up."

"Huh?" he asked, not immediately grasping my problem.

"I can't stand," I said, gripping the handicap rail, desperately trying to pull my body to its feet. My legs were encased in cement, my muscles refusing to work.

"This isn't right," Chris worried, lifting me to my feet.

"You think?" I snapped, shuffling back to the bed, my husband supporting the bulk of my weight. If I kept my knees locked I could almost walk, but as soon as they bent, my legs crumbled.

I could tell by the anxious faces that everyone was deeply concerned, but I refused to let on that there was truly something wrong with my body. "I'm fine," I said icily, attempting to abolish their looks of pity. But as I struggled to lift my battered body back into bed, I secretly wondered if I would ever be normal again.

CHAPTER TEN

At eight p.m., nearly seven hours after she first arrived, Chris and I were finally alone with our daughter again. The grandparents had said their final goodbyes, taken their last pictures, and rocked their little doll one more time.

A new nurse came on shift. She looked like she was trying not to gag whenever she walked into our room.

"I'll take her whenever you're ready, no hurry," she muttered with downcast eyes, expressionless. She quickly checked my vitals and left.

We decided to have an autopsy performed on Avery, even though the cause of death appeared to be the tightly wrapped umbilical cord. After talking with the doctors, we wanted ensure the accident with the cord wasn't masking a larger issue that could be repeated in subsequent pregnancies. We wanted to get all the answers we could, to leave no stone unturned. Yet our decision made it even more difficult to let Avery go, knowing that when we did we were sending her perfect little body off to a cold metal slab to be dissected like a science project.

Time is not kind to the dead. Avery still looked beautiful, but her body had grown cold and rigormortis was rapidly setting in. Her fingers, once warm and pliable, resisted my touch, and I feared breaking them when I tried to hold her hand. Her rosy skin had taken on the purple tone of death. But I still wasn't ready to say goodbye.

"I can't leave her yet," I whined to Chris. "I'm not ready."

"We can wait," he replied. He wasn't ready, either.

"But we can't keep her all night, can we? They said to keep her as long as we wanted, but I think they meant hours, not days, right?"

"Probably," Chris answered, slumping in his chair. He had come into the hospital looking strong and healthy, but the past forty-eight hours had not been kind. I was thankful the only mirror was in the bathroom so we didn't have to constantly stare at the ghosts we had become.

We sat in silence, something that was becoming unnervingly normal, staring at our dead baby. We were tired of talking, tired of thinking, tired of forcing smiles and being polite. We were tired of the hospital, tired of making decisions, tired of the chaos our perfectly ordinary life had become.

We wanted normal again.

We would never know normal again.

As the evening dragged on, the summer sky turned a deep purple, a blazing red streak of sun carving a path toward the horizon. It was breathtaking, a fiery ending to a hellish day. Before long our room turned dark, with the exception of a small fluorescent light in the far corner. An eerie orange glow illuminated the sterile walls.

"Can you get her for me?" I asked my husband, using the controls to elevate the back of my bed. I still wasn't able to walk independently.

Chris slowly left the chair that had been his post for the last two days. He shuffled to the bassinette, hunched over like a withered old man.

As Avery fell into my arms for the third and final time, I was devastated by the chill of her body. When she was warm, my baby girl was really there. Now she finally felt what she was.

Dead.

I tried to pretend she was simply asleep, but without her warmth she was so different, so cold and motionless, a shell of a human being. She was just a vessel for something greater that was already gone. I knew my daughter wasn't really there, but holding that tiny body was the only way I had to say goodbye.

Chris left Avery's swaddling blanket in the bassinet, and I stared at the stiff pink cotton dress the nurse had dressed her in. It was old-fashioned, borderline ugly, with a high, white lace collar. It made her look even more doll-like. I carefully placed my shaking fingers on the high neckline and took a deep breath. I pulled the lace down and stared hard at the discolored ring around my daughter's neck, the bruised circle that told the tragic story of her death. I gently traced the line with my fingers, wondering how life could be so cruel.

I cursed myself for not bringing something special for her to wear. I thought of the gorgeous white crocheted dress hanging in Avery's closet, handmade by a family friend, and wished I'd told Chris to bring it with him to the hospital. Avery would have looked so beautiful in that dress, like an angel. Like the angel she had become.

I kissed my daughter's forehead, then her button nose, and grabbed her tiny hands one last time, wondering how I was going to live without her in my life.

"I think I'm ready," I whispered to Chris, hot, salty tears spilling down my cheeks.

"Okay," he said, standing, waiting to retrieve her.

As he reached to take her I pulled her closer to my chest. "Wait," I howled, hugging my daughter's rigid body. "I just…I just need one more minute."

I held her in my arms and rocked her back and forth, savoring the last time I would ever see my daughter in the flesh. Tears blinded me as I showered her tiny fingers with wet kisses, warming her cold skin with my own blistering tears.

"I love her so much," I sobbed, unable to let go. "I just love her so much."

"I know," Chris whispered, turning away from my pain.

"I'm so sorry, Avery," I sobbed. "I'm so sorry, so sorry."

I snorted, swiftly wiping my tears away, trying to regain my composure.

"Okay," I inhaled. "Okay, I'm ready. Call the nurse."

"Are you sure?"

"No. But if I don't do it now I won't do it at all."

As Chris did as I asked, I stared hard at my daughter for the final time, desperately trying to burn her image into my mind. The flat feet, the button nose, the skinny knees…I wanted to be sure that in the future I could simply close my eyes and see my baby girl exactly as she had been. I never wanted to forget.

Chris sat down on the edge of the bed and took Avery's free hand.

"Goodbye, Avery," he whispered, kissing her fingers. "Daddy loves you."

Another wave of tears filled my eyes as the nurse entered the room carrying a wicker Moses basket. She walked to the bedside and waited silently.

I kissed Avery one last time and looked at the nurse. "We're ready." I smiled through my tears, handing over my only child.

The solemn woman forced a reciprocal smile and took my daughter into her arms, silently carrying her to the other side of the room. Chris and I watched gravely as she removed the knit hat and the pink dress, folding them neatly. The room was dim, but I could see tears in the woman's eyes as she quickly wrapped Avery in a blanket and tucked her tiny body into the basket.

That was the last time I saw my daughter.

"If you need anything else tonight, let me know," she whispered, closing the door. It was the farthest from me Avery had ever been.

I thought of a ceramic plaque I'd once seen in a gift shop that read, "Having a baby is to decide forever to have your heart go walking around outside your body." I finally understood what that meant as I watched my heart walk out the door.

I wanted to yell "Stop," to jump out of bed and tackle the evil woman who had just stolen my daughter, but instead I sat there, staring blankly, frozen, numb, feeling the aching void in my chest where my heart had once been.

"I don't know if I'm ready," I mumbled. I looked at Chris, silently asking him to fix this.

"I can go get the nurse, tell her to bring her back," he offered. I knew he meant it. At that point he was willing to do anything for me.

I considered his proposal and was very close to agreeing when what little logic I had left took over. "I'm never going to be ready," I sniffed. "If she comes back I don't know if I'll be able to give her up again. It's not like we can just take Avery home with us..."

Although I really wanted to.

Chris settled back in his chair, reaching for the remote to turn on the TV.

"Let's just go to bed," I sighed, burying my head under a blanket. It smelled vaguely of hospital disinfectant and made my head ache.

"Goodnight," Chris said, brushing his lips across my cheek.

"Goodnight," I replied, burying my face in a pillow. I expected sleep to elude me, to toss and turn and to be haunted by the tragic events consuming my life. But within minutes the sweet blackness crept into my brain and sleep took over.

I slept like the dead.

*****

I awoke with the sun at six a.m. Pain surged through my body. My back ached from three nights in a hospital bed, but that wasn't the primary source of my discomfort. As I came to I considered the stitches in my ass, my raging hemorrhoid, and the inability to walk, but still couldn't pinpoint the epicenter of this new pain.

"Uhhh," I moaned, poking my chest. My boobs felt hot and tight, like two overstuffed balloons bursting with scalding water.

"What's wrong?" Chris yawned, rubbing the sleep from his eyes.

"I think my milk's come in," I groaned miserably, flashing him a peek of my inflated breasts.

His sullen face turned boyish. "Your boobs are huge," he blurted, reaching across the bed to grab one.

"I don't think so," I clucked, slapping his hand away. Men.

Along with the pain, my bloated boobs depressed me even more; they were another reminder of what I had lost. I was supposed to be happily feeding my baby with those huge milk bags, not cursing them and wondering how long it would take for them to dry up.

I thought of Rose of Sharon in *The Grapes of Wrath*, the young woman who feeds the starving man with her breast milk after the death of her baby. We read that novel my first year of teaching, and I'd discussed the significance of that scene with a bunch of squirming eleventh-graders. I never in a million years thought I would have anything in common with a Steinbeck character.

A new nurse arrived, one I recognized vaguely from my extended stay, but all of the faces were blending together. She administered another dose of IV antibiotics and took my vitals.

"The doctor should be in to see you sometime this morning." She smiled cheerily. "I think they're going to let you go home today, if you want."

Home. I had forgotten home existed. I thought of the blood-spattered carpet in our bedroom and the cherry cradle placed next to my bed. I pictured Avery's finished nursery eagerly awaiting an occupant, filled with books to be read and teddy bears to be hugged. Her closet was overflowing with pretty pink clothes on tiny pink hangers that would never be worn.

We not only had a house full of reminders—we also had a house full of people. My mother and Chris's parents were waiting for us there, undoubtedly anxious to help us sweep up the pieces of our shattered life. I looked around the room, trying to decide if going home was really what I wanted.

I hated that hospital room.

"Good," I finally answered, if half-heartedly. "It'll be nice to be home."

An hour later the lone female doctor in the practice, my favorite of the three, entered my room. It was the first time she had seen me since Avery's birth.

"I'm so, so sorry," she said, giving me a hug. I could see the sorrow in her eyes, and I knew that she genuinely meant it. She went on to relay how they were all deeply saddened by the news of Avery and how the whole office was thinking of me. It was such a terrible accident.

She proceeded to ask me a handful of questions to gauge my level of depression. I answered them almost jovially, partly because that's my nature, but mostly because I was determined to avoid seeing a psychiatrist or being stuck in the hospital for another day.

Satisfied with my answers, she explained what would happen to my body, from the hormonal shifts and the bleeding to how to make my milk dry up faster.

Finally, as she finished with the medical details, she grabbed my hand and sighed, tears welling in her eyes.

"You are a mother," she said, looking me straight in the eye. "You had a child, and you are a mother. Do not let anyone tell you differently."

I wrestled with my tears as she continued to look at me. The words were difficult to hear, but I needed them. It was the first time anyone had called me a mother; it was the first time I had felt like a mother. The past few days had left me confused and unsure of my identity. I didn't know if I was supposed to brush Avery under the rug and pretend she never happened or embrace the fact that I had brought a beautiful life into the world, if only for a moment.

"Okay," I sniffed. "Okay."

"All right," she said. "Let's see if we can get you out of here by noon."

She finished up her examination and left, giving me one last hug and demanding I make an appointment to see her after the weekend.

I had to wait for one more round of IV antibiotics before I was free, but I managed a shower with a plastic bag on my arm. My legs were still weak; Chris waited in the bathroom with me to make sure I didn't collapse.

We had asked every doctor and nurse that entered our room about my legs, but no one had a definite answer. The general consensus was that, due to my extended time pushing, I had blown out the muscles and overstretched the ligaments in my knees and quadriceps. My legs would eventually heal with exercise and time.

I did my hair, put on makeup, and examined my face in the mirror. I looked like I'd been through hell, but the dark circles were a little lighter and my skin slightly pinker. I no longer looked like a corpse.

I had a breakdown getting dressed, when I realized the only clothes that fit me were maternity clothes.

"I still look pregnant," I groaned, throwing an ill-fitting shirt on the floor. "I don't have a baby, but I still look pregnant."

I buried my head in my hands and took a deep breath. Part of me really thought I could go home and forget the whole experience, but my swollen post-baby body was just another reminder. Every roll and every extra ounce of fat was going to drive home Avery's loss. I stared dejectedly at my naked stomach. A day earlier it had been huge and hard. Now it was sad and jiggly, empty and soft.

I hastily picked up my belongings and packed my bags. We were given a beautiful blue, handcrafted wooden memory box that held Avery's hat, dress, a tiny angel pin, and a hospital bracelet labeled "Baby Girl Chandler." It also contained the standard hospital-issue certificate listing our daughter's birth date, time, length, and weight, with her tiny hand- and footprints captured in black ink. Our final parting gift was a small clay mold of Avery's tiny hands. It was the closest I'd ever get to holding her hand again.

One thing we didn't receive was a birth certificate. In the state of Michigan a stillborn baby never lived, and therefore it cannot be born. I beg to differ, as I felt my daughter live inside of me each and every day—but to the state, Avery never existed. It hurt me to think that my daughter would never be recognized as an actual human being and would never be named by anybody other than me.

I finished packing and sat down again. I felt like a kid on the last day of school before summer break, impatiently awaiting release from my temporary confinement. I couldn't wait for that final bell, for sweet freedom, to run around barefoot in the sunlight without a care in the world.

The day's nurse appeared, holding a stack of papers. "Don't get too excited. I don't have the discharge papers yet."

She handed me the papers, a bunch of different brochures and Xeroxed handouts titled "Coping with Loss" and "Dealing with Grief." She handed Chris one that read "A Man's Guide to Loss."

I stared at the brochures, stifling a maniacal giggle. My daughter died, and this was the advice they had to offer? I opened up the blue one, "Dealing with Grief."

The first lines stared back and me, big and bold: *It's okay to be sad.*

Really? It was okay for me to be sad? That made me feel so much better about sending my only child to a crematorium.

I pretended to listen as the nurse gave us an overview of the information and encouraged us to read everything thoroughly.

She finally informed us that Avery's autopsy would be performed that afternoon. Her body would be sent to the funeral home that evening.

"The funeral home will be calling you to make arrangements," she explained on her way out.

I was happy Avery was still in the building, close to her parents, but I imagined her lying in the basement morgue on a metal slab, cold, scared, and alone, waiting to be cut open by a stranger. It shouldn't be that way. She should be with us.

"I wish we could go see her again," I whispered, more to myself than to Chris.

We were finally discharged shortly before noon. Chris took our bags down to the car and returned with a wheelchair.

"Really?" I laughed, staring at the wheelchair.

"They made me take it. They say it's hospital protocol." He shrugged. "Besides, it's not like you can walk."

"Shut up," I retorted, locking my knees and slowly tottering toward the chair.

As Chris wheeled me to the elevator, the nurses went about their business; no one stopped to say goodbye or wish us well. I wasn't sure if they were too busy or just happy to see the pariahs of the maternity ward finally leave. I waved goodbye to no one in particular as the elevator doors closed.

Moving through the lobby of the birthing center was a strange, unsettling feeling. It was the first time I had been around people in four days, and I was rolling through a dream. Relatives of happy new moms were eating lunch and chatting, some carrying flowers with giant balloons that announced "It's a boy!" or "It's a girl!" A few glanced at me; most did not. Everyone looked so damn happy.

I hated all of them.

And then there was me: miserable, twenty-four hours removed from giving birth to a beautiful baby girl, leaving the hospital with empty arms. It was supposed to be a joyous occasion, my day, Avery's day, with strangers smiling and cooing over the beautiful pink bundle tucked safely in my arms. Instead I was invisible in a sea of people, a fat girl in a wheelchair awkwardly clutching a brown leather purse.

I suppressed the urge to scream. "I just had a baby, too!" I shouted in my head. "She's dead down in the basement, waiting for her autopsy."

I wondered how many days I'd ruin with that.

I sucked in my anger and kept my mouth shut. I was determined not to lose my mind. Not in public, anyway.

Chris helped me into the car and hurried to the driver's seat. "I can't wait to get away from this fucking place," he scowled, putting the car in drive.

I nodded in agreement but couldn't hold back my tears.

"What's wrong?" he asked, shifting the car back to park.

I stared longingly at the building we both despised. "I know it's stupid," I began. "But I feel like we're just abandoning her. We're just leaving her there, all alone. I know we can't take her with us, but how can we just leave her there? She's our baby. She's supposed to come home with us. And we're just leaving her..."

Chris squeezed my hand as I sobbed. But there was nothing we could do but leave.

I looked back at the hospital one final time and said a silent goodbye to my baby girl.

CHAPTER ELEVEN

Our living room looked like a funeral home. Word traveled fast, and over a dozen floral arrangements and waxy-leaved plants blanketed the house. The smell was pungent and borderline nauseating.

Every sign of Avery had been hidden away in her bedroom, the door to the nursery closed, the bloody carpet in my bedroom painstakingly scrubbed. The only reminder that anything out of the ordinary had happened was the flora and fauna blanketing every surface.

As I hobbled through my home, I was treated to an onslaught of heartfelt hugs and a chorus of "How are you feeling?" from our parents. Everywhere I went I had a permanent shadow; there was always someone one step behind me, eager to attend to my every need. I knew their intentions were good, but their constant presence made me even more irritable.

A single card rested on our kitchen island, waiting to be opened. I stared at it, afraid of what I might find inside. My hands shook as I ripped the seal. It was from our neighbors across the street, a sweet older couple we barely knew.

It was a generic Audubon Society card with two birds on the front, a card reserved for quick thank-yous or impromptu hellos.

I noticed it was dated Wednesday, July 2.

Avery's birthday.

Dear Heidi & Chris,
I just heard the news and wanted you to know that we
are thinking about you. I hope you find strength and love
from your family and friends at this very sad time. Know
that we are here if you need anything.
Love, Your Neighbors, John & Linda

I sucked in a sob as I returned the card to the envelope, unsure why their kind words made me want to cry.

"How did they know already?" I asked, amazed.

"We saw the wife when we were getting the mail," my mother-in-law explained. "She saw the extra cars and figured you had the baby."

"Oh," was all I could think to say. I wandered around the room, looking at the cards on our new greenery. Most of the arrangements were from my husband's coworkers and suppliers. One was from his softball team, and my brother sent a giant peace lily. I was honored that Avery had touched so many, but it made me sad that so many people already knew. For me it was a personal tragedy, my tragedy, and I felt violated that so many strangers were aware of my pain. I wondered what the reactions were when all these people, many whom I did not know, had heard the news of my daughter's death.

I grabbed my hospital-issued ass-donut and slowly walked from the kitchen to the living room. Chris, his parents, and my mother were sitting the couch, watching TV, making small talk. I tried to be social but couldn't bear it. After twenty minutes of sitting, my giant hemorrhoid ached and my head throbbed from the trivial conversation.

Everyone's eyes were on me as I stood, using the arm of the couch for leverage. I desperately wanted to tell everyone to get the hell out of my house, to leave me alone—that this was my time to grieve, and they were interrupting the process.

Instead I forced a half-smile and yawned. "I'm going to go lie down," I explained, pointing to our bedroom. "Maybe take a shower or something."

My words were met with silent stares as I gimped toward my bedroom, thanking our builder for putting it on the first floor. Wondering eyes burned a hole in my back.

"Do you need any help?" someone asked.

"I'm fine," I answered bitterly, slamming the door.

In my room I found my cat Nina, the old lady I'd had for twelve years. She stretched out on the bed and yawned, looking at me expectantly.

Without any leg strength it took a few tries to heave my wounded body into our tall sleigh bed, but I eventually made it. I curled up on my side and faced the windows.

It was yet another painstakingly beautiful July day. The windows were open, the smell of summer floating in the air. Nina curled up against my chest; together we watched the leaves dance in the breeze. It was a happy day, the kind meant for barbecues and bike rides and flying kites, and it just made me more depressed.

I thought of Avery and tried to make sense of what had happened, to understand what in this universe had wanted her to die, but my brain refused to function. I fell into a trance; all I could do was stare out the window and stroke my cat. I wanted to cry but couldn't. I wanted to scream but had no voice. I had been sad before, but this was different. I felt dead inside. Suddenly my life, which had always been so full of happiness and joy, was no longer worth living.

I had no idea how to make that feeling go away.

Nina, now the closest thing I had to a child, consoled me for the next two hours. She nuzzled and purred, telling me it would be okay in her feline way, giving the unconditional love that only animals are capable of giving. She didn't take my pain away, but she managed to temporarily make me feel needed and loved, which in turn made me feel a little more alive. I don't know if she sensed how much I needed her, but I will be forever grateful for the affection of that cat.

I would have spent the rest of the day in bed if my bladder hadn't forced me up. Leaving the bed was difficult, but I managed to make it to the toilet in our attached master bath. As I sat down to pee I realized that I had failed to anticipate a potential problem: our bathroom didn't have handicapped rails, and there was nothing I could use for leverage to pull myself up.

I was officially stuck on the toilet.

I spent five minutes of pure frustration trying to get up, but my legs were too weak. I could either wait until someone came and checked on me or swallow my pride and scream for help.

"Chris," I yelled meekly, hoping he could hear me.

Silence.

"Chris?" I shouted a little louder. I prayed no one else came in his place.

Silence.

I tried one last time. "Chris!" I screamed, fighting back tears. I hated feeling helpless, and I cursed the trials that had put me here.

I finally heard the door to the bedroom open.

"What? Are you okay?" I heard panic in his voice. "Where are you?"

"In here," I muttered as he entered the bathroom.

He almost cracked a smile but thought better of it as he read the torment on my face.

"I can't get up," I said.

"What do you mean you can't get up?"

"I can't get up. I tried. I've been trying for five minutes."

Chris grabbed my arm and slowly lifted me to my feet. "Maybe we should go to the doctor," he said. "This isn't normal."

"It will get better," I replied. "It just needs time." I had to believe that. Besides, after four days in the hospital, the last thing I wanted to do was go back to the doctor.

Chris stared at me as I turned on the shower.

I stared back and pointed at the shower stall. "I'm going to shower. Is that okay with you?"

"Do you want me to wait?"

"No, why would you do that?"

"In case you fall or something. I'm worried."

"Just go. I'll be fine."

Chris reluctantly left the room, leaving me with a quick kiss on the forehead. He insisted on cracking the door "just in case." I obliged, partly out of respect for my husband and partly out of my own fear that something might go wrong. Alone, I slowly undressed, making sure I didn't put too much weight on my legs. I cautiously stepped into the hot shower, careful not to let the water hit my swollen breasts. The last thing I needed was to flow like a dairy cow.

I gazed at the beige walls, the fiberglass floor. Just days before I stood in the exact same place, pregnant, horrified by the blood surging between my legs. Back then I still had hope; back then I believed whatever had happened was fixable and my daughter would be okay.

I closed my eyes and tried to shake the memories, to erase the frantic scene that kept replaying in my head.

I rested my forehead against the cool tile wall as the steaming water drenched my back, washing away any remnants of the hospital. I felt safe in my solitude, finally able to let go of my festering anger. Tears crashed through me, mingling with the spray from the showerhead, and I found myself blindly clutching the tile walls with my fingers, grasping for stability in my sorrow. The word "why" silently fell from my trembling lips, drowned out by the sound of rushing water. I began convulsing, great sobs engulfing my body. For the first time since I was told Avery was dead, I let down my guard and allowed myself to mourn. I wanted to curl up into a ball on the shower floor, to let the water wash me down the drain, but standing was my only option—I would never be able to make it back up.

The shower became my sanctuary, a place where no one could bother me or hear my cries. I wept for fifteen minutes, then an internal switch flipped and the waterworks ceased. I wanted to spend the rest of my life standing under the water, but I knew my family would worry if I didn't emerge from my hiding place.

I reluctantly turned the water off and opened the shower door; Chris instantly appeared at my side. For a moment I felt betrayed, like my solitude was an illusion and he had been listening to my meltdown through the cracked door. But if he had, he didn't let on as he helped me towel off. I dressed in a pair of flannel pajama pants (meticulously pulled on one leg at a time to avoid falling) and an old white Cabo San Lucas t-shirt, the only non-maternity clothes I felt comfortable in. I put on enough makeup to not look like a zombie, and Chris once again left me alone.

I was about to crawl back in bed when the phone rang. I heard Chris answer it on the second ring. His voice grew louder as he walked down the hall toward our room. "It's Nicky," he mouthed. Nicky was my best friend, the closest thing I had to a sister. She lived two hours away and had been calling daily to get news on Avery's pending arrival; she was oblivious to the events of the last few days.

I sat in silence as my husband gave my best friend the short version of what had happened, from my water breaking in the middle of the night to the cord being wrapped around Avery's neck twice. I was thankful he was doing my dirty work, saving me the agony of having to tell Nicky our terrible story. Then Chris handed me the phone.

I blinked, surprised that he expected me to talk. I stared at the receiver held out in front of my face and reluctantly grabbed it from my husband's hand.

"Hi there," I said, doing my best to sound like myself.

"Oh my God," Nicky cried. "Heidi, I'm so sorry, oh my God, how...oh my God..."

She was clearly in shock, and it became my job to console her.

"Well, you know, these things happen sometimes," I began, trying to sound optimistic. "It's not that common, but I guess it happens. But I'm okay. Really, I am."

"I...I don't..." Nicky started, words failing her. "I'll call you back."

Click.

I sat on the bed and stared at the phone. I couldn't blame her for not knowing what to say. It had happened to me—I had been there—yet it was impossible even for me to process. As I handed the phone back to Chris my heart sank a little, for I knew that was just the first of many awkward conversations I would have about my daughter.

Nicky called back an hour later, much more composed and apologetic. Her voice kept cracking, and I could hear genuine sadness in her words. She wanted to know every detail, and I felt like I was explaining a movie plot as I narrated my story. Avery's story. I had lived it, but I still felt like an outsider looking in on someone else's tragic tale.

"So how are you guys doing?" I asked, attempting normal conversation. But the talk kept shifting back to Avery.

The rest of the afternoon was uneventful save for a few floral deliveries. Chris mowed the lawn and did household chores. I spent the hours in my room, resentful that he could physically and mentally lose himself in such ordinary tasks, as both my body and mind were destroyed.

For most of the afternoon my in-laws sat on the deck in the sunshine with my mother, sipping iced tea, reading magazines, and talking. I could hear them outside my window as they chatted, sometimes talking of the weather, sometimes talking of Avery. Occasionally they laughed. Their words were muffled yet deafening; I wanted them to disappear, to go back to their lives and let me live mine in silence.

I thought of the old saying about houseguests: they're like fish, and after a few days they start to stink. My house smelled like a Goddamn fish market.

As the sun went down I knew I needed to show my face or resign myself to an unwanted interrogation about my mental state. I emerged from my haven and shuffled around the house, carrying a donut for my smoldering ass, trying to assimilate into the land of the living.

I hoped no one would notice I was lost in the land of the dead.

*****

I awoke Friday morning amazed at how well I'd slept. In those glorious seconds that separate sleep from consciousness, Avery's death was somehow forgotten. In those seconds, she was safe inside my belly or playing quietly in her crib. For an instant, the darkness was gone, and I had a taste of happiness.

And then I remembered.

Chris threw his arm around me, and we held each other silently in the pale morning light. It was yet another beautiful day with abundant sunshine and happy, chirping birds singing outside my window. The sheer white curtains billowed softly, kissed by the gentle breeze.

I wished it would rain.

"I hate waking up," I growled, turning to face Chris. "I hate having to remember all over again."

He lifted his strong hand and began stroking my tousled blond bedhead. "Me too," he replied, yawning, his eyes drifting to a faraway place.

We spent as much time as we could in bed, mostly in silence, until Chris finally got up to face our houseguests. He caught me rubbing my belly as he dressed. "It's getting smaller," he said optimistically.

I stared at my stomach, still bloated and foreign-looking. "It's weird thinking it's empty," I sighed, squeezing the stretched-out blob that once housed a human being.

I forced myself to get out of bed, gingerly using the stepstool Chris insisted on placing on my side. My dad was driving down that day, and I was both happy and sad to see him. I was happy because I could hug him; I was sad because I knew it was heartbreaking for the people who loved me most to witness my pain.

The morning was dreadfully boring. We had breakfast; everyone else read books and went for walks and did mundane chores. I spent most of my time in the upstairs office on the computer. The first thing I did was email my boss, the school principal, explaining what had happened. I asked him to relay the information to my colleagues. I dreaded sending the email and half thought if I ignored Avery's death people might forget I'd been pregnant by the time a new school year rolled around.

I read the email one last time, took a deep breath, and clicked Send. Now a whole new sector of my life would mourn for me, and the next onslaught of flowers and cards and well-wishes would trickle in. People would naturally question what happened; whispers and rumors would begin. Once again I found myself wondering how many would blame me for letting my daughter die. How could they not? I was.

I wrote a separate email to our close friends providing a more detailed explanation of Avery's death, hoping to avoid picking up the phone for a while. It was the Fourth of July, and I knew most of them were enjoying a long weekend with family and friends, relaxing and barbecuing and sipping cocktails, putting the worries of the real world away for a few splendid days. I thought of the shock they would experience when they read my message and silently apologized for ruining their days.

With both messages hurtling through cyberspace, I sat staring at the computer, trying to figure out my next move. I had work to do, as I needed to finish up the last of the high school yearbook I'd failed to complete before going into labor, but my brain took me elsewhere. I found myself staring at the Google search box, where I mindlessly typed the word "stillbirth."

In an instant I was bombarded with over two million results and a handful of images that forced me to close my eyes, pictures of other people's dead children posted for all the world to see. I rubbed my tired eyes and opened them again, clicking on the first thing I saw, the Wikipedia definition.

"A stillbirth occurs when a fetus has died in the uterus. The Australian definition specifies that fetal death is termed a stillbirth after twenty weeks gestation or the fetus weighs more than four hundred grams (fourteen ounces). Once the fetus has died, the mother still has contractions and remains undelivered. The term is often used in distinction to live birth or miscarriage. Most stillbirths occur in full-term pregnancies."

I glanced through the rest of the information, tempted to add to the definition: "A stillbirth tears out your heart and rips it to shreds right before your eyes. The Heidi definition specifies that never in your life will you feel so useless and alone. Once your baby has died, you will no longer have a reason to live."

I stared at the page for another minute and exited the browser, turning to the unfinished pages of the 2008 Lakeview High School yearbook. It took a while to focus, but once I did it was bizarrely liberating to work on something so trivial in the throes of the biggest crisis of my life. I began to understand why Chris had buried himself in work.

As I edited pages for spelling and grammar, I was remiss, wondering who really gave a fuck if a sentence ended with a preposition. I stopped for a moment on the prom page, staring at the tan, smiling faces of teenagers playing dress-up, completely engrossed in the drama of their own sheltered little worlds. They had no idea what the real world was like; they had no idea what real pain was. I sighed, wondering how many of them would experience authentic heartache by the time they were my age.

For the first time in days the hours flew. My task was monotonous, but it felt good to lose myself in something other than my own misery. I wasn't ready to stop yet when I ran out of pages, so I went through the last few again, hoping to make more work for myself. Unable to uncover any additional errors, I cursed the efficiency of my students and reluctantly headed back to reality.

My confidence walking had grown, partly with my own denial. I refused to believe that my once-athletic legs could possibly be forever ruined, and, like any athlete, I was going to push myself. I'd made it up the stairs to the office on my own, so I didn't think twice about going down unassisted. It was tough, and I relied heavily on the banister for support, but I managed it.

Until I reached the last four stairs.

In an instant my weakened body buckled, and I tumbled to the bottom in a grunting heap. The giant thud brought people running from all directions; I could hear Chris chastising me in the distance for not asking for help.

I tumbled twice and landed square on my ass; the pain was excruciating, like I'd fallen into a raging bonfire and my backside was going up in flames. I'd torn during delivery, leaving me with stitches and a giant, burning hemorrhoid. I couldn't even sit on a plush couch, and now I had torn my ass even farther apart. Chris helped me to my feet, and we rushed to the bathroom to see if there was fresh blood.

"Shit. I know I ripped my stitches," I moaned, pulling off my pants. I looked at the crotch of my cotton panties and found fresh blood splatter. "Oh God, I don't want to go back to the hospital."

"Are you sure you ripped them?" he asked, looking at the blood.

"I don't know, I can't tell," I replied. "I can't really see down there."

"Do you want me to check them for you?" a voice asked. My mother had made her way into the room.

Although my mother was a doctor, and I knew she'd seen it all, the last thing I wanted was to have her inspecting my throbbing, bleeding vagina.

"No thanks, it's fine," I said, giving her a look that told her to get the hell out.

She surprisingly respected my wishes, and as my mother disappeared, Chris whispered, "Do you want me to check it? I mean, I don't want to look down there, but if you really think you ripped them..."

It was the only option I could think of other than the emergency room. I climbed pantsless on the bed and spread my legs wide while my poor husband inspected my torn privates with a flashlight. I seriously wondered if he regretted marrying me.

"Oh God, this isn't pretty," he grumbled, staring at my crotch. "I don't know if I'm ever going to be able to go down here again."

He sat up, and I couldn't help but giggle at the look on his face. "They look okay," he said, revolted. "Disgusting, but okay. I don't think you ripped them. But promise me you'll never make me do that again." I slapped him lightly across the cheek and laughed, the realest laugh I'd had in close to a week.

My dad arrived after lunch. He presented me with an extra-long hug and a cane, an old gold and wooden thing my grandpa had picked up at a garage sale. I looked away when I saw the tears glistening in his eyes; I was used to making people smile, and I hated that I was doing the opposite.

The stubborn side of me didn't want to use the cane—that would be admitting my helplessness—but I couldn't deny that it made walking easier. Before long I was cruising around the house like an old pro, and I felt almost normal physically if I stayed away from the stairs. I became more alive with my newfound mobility.

More flowers arrived; a stack of sympathy cards came in the mail. I absentmindedly opened the top one, unaware that sympathy cards would make me cry like a baby.

Nothing can compare with the loss of one you've dreamed of and cared about...

A terrible sob escaped my throat as I stared at the blue words etched on turquoise cardstock. My body chilled as I opened the card.

Though it's difficult to express all the sympathy that goes out to you at this time, I still hope you know how close you are in heart and thought today.

It was from a friend of my parents, someone I hadn't seen in years.

It wasn't anything spectacular, yet the words echoed in my head. Nothing can compare with the loss of one you've dreamed of and cared about...I suddenly saw Avery's face, her fingers. Her smell wafted through my nose. No, nothing could compare with my loss. I had been through hell, and people felt bad about it. But other people's sympathy didn't change anything.

I quickly tried to brush my tears away before anyone noticed and placed the other cards in a basket on the kitchen counter. If reading sympathy cards made me an emotional wreck, I certainly wasn't going to do it in a house full of people. I would save those condolences for another time, a time when I was stronger or a time when I simply didn't care if I broke down. I didn't want anyone else trying to clean me up.

Yet I was still troubled by my intense reaction to the card. For some reason kind words from friends, acquaintances, and people I barely knew caused my grief to boil over. In expressing their grief, they caused me to re-examine my own sorrow, to remember all over again how monumental a thing I had lost.

There wasn't anything to celebrate, but it was the Fourth of July, and someone convinced me to leave the house and take our boat out on the lake. It was surreal pulling up to the slip and seeing the shimmering water, something that represented fun and happiness. The last time I'd been on the Big Banana I had been full of life, my belly ready to burst. I closed my eyes and pictured myself lounging in the front of the boat in my sunglasses, my hair tied in a bun, inevitable stray pieces blowing in the wind. My black maternity bathing suit was a little too tight; I was reading a parenting magazine and chugging a giant bottle of water to stay hydrated. It had been less than a week, but it seemed so long ago—a different time, a different life.

I opened my eyes and looked at myself, puffy and awkward, wearing ill-fitting boxer shorts and a tank top that hugged the jiggling rolls of my belly in all the wrong places, limping along the seawall with my cane. I prayed we didn't see anyone we knew.

Being forced outside was supposed to make me feel better, but it only made me feel worse. I was detached from the world, from my life. I didn't know which way was up and which was down, and I really didn't give a shit. I was counting the minutes until I could crawl back inside my hole and be alone.

Everyone we passed looked so damn happy; every boat was loaded up with the cutest little kids. I was jealous of their freedom, their families, of their untroubled existence. It was a joyous holiday for everyone else, a time to enjoy the sunshine and relax. But for me it was two days after my daughter died. That's all it was and all that it could be.

We spent an hour cruising the lake; I sat in the front alone, soaking up late-day sun and hating the world. Chris steered as our parents ogled the million-dollar mansions dotting the shore.

"What a nice afternoon," someone said from the back of the boat.

"I know," someone else agreed. "It's beautiful."

My daughter was fucking beautiful, I thought, grinding my teeth in anger. How could they just sit back and relax like they didn't have a care in the world?

After docking we drove the short distance back to our house. Our parents continued to lament what a beautiful day it was, how perfect the lake was, and how nice it was to finally get out of the house. I wanted to slap them all. They could get out of my house any time they fucking felt like it. But I bit my lip and looked out the window instead.

CHAPTER TWELVE

By Sunday we were finally alone. Visitors trickled in to pay their respects; while I appreciated the thought, "entertaining" was mind numbing. I looked and felt like I had been hit by a truck, and I loathed trying to smile and pretend I was okay. I hated the pity in people's eyes when they looked at me. I know that's what happens in a tragedy—people feel bad for you—but it only made me feel worse about myself.

A few people asked what Avery looked like. I was tempted to get out the pictures from our hospital photo shoot, but I was afraid people would find them revolting. Instead I described her curly black hair, her almond eyes, the button nose and rosy lips. I was taken aback when one friend, a coworker, actually asked if I had any pictures.

I studied her carefully, unsure what she was asking. "Yes, we took a few at the hospital."

"Do you mind if I see them?" she asked. "If you don't want me to, I understand."

I walked slowly to my bedroom, opened the blue keepsake box from the hospital, and grabbed a stack of photos. I felt a curious rush of excitement as she quietly thumbed through the pictures of my daughter, spending a great deal of time examining each one. Tears formed in the corner of her eyes.

"She's beautiful," she whispered, flashing a sympathetic smile.

As she handed back the stack of pictures, my heart was bursting with joy. Having someone else look at Avery, someone who wasn't family or medical staff, validated her existence.

I did have a daughter, and she was beautiful. I needed to remember that.

Most of our visitors were gracious and polite, careful not to say too much or stay too long. They waited for us to do the talking, unsure of what to say about such a sensitive situation. There were a few, though—as there always are, I suppose—who said all the wrong things. One friend blurted, "Well, at least you can have another one." It was true, as far as I knew, that I could have another baby, but was that supposed to make me feel better about the one I lost? Avery was not a dog that ran away; she was a human being, a person I had loved and bonded with. She could not and would not ever be replaced by the birth of another child.

A friend with a (living) child said, "I don't understand what happened. How did you not know something was wrong? I mean, couldn't you tell she wasn't moving? I always felt my baby move."

The words pierced my heart and haunted me every second of every day. I replayed that question over and over and over again, and the only conclusion I ever came to was that it was my fault. I was already paranoid that people blamed me for what happened, and her words reinforced that.

I couldn't stand the people who said it was "God's plan" or "God wanted it this way." I wasn't the most religious person in the world, but I believed in God, and I refused to accept the idea that God stole my daughter for a reason. That was a lame excuse for her death, and if "God really wanted it this way," then God could go straight to hell.

As the weekend came and went in a blur, Chris decided to work from home for the coming week. His company graciously granted him all the time he needed to grieve, but I knew he wanted to leave the house and go back to work. Our house was a constant reminder of death, the silence a reminder that there was no baby. It was strange; our home was the same as it always had been, yet entirely different. Even though Avery never lived outside of my womb, our home still missed her presence.

I told Chris I would be fine without him, that he should just go to the office, but he maintained that he didn't trust me home alone. He wasn't worried I was depressed and might attempt suicide, because I was actually holding it together quite well—on the outside, at least. The main reason he stayed was my legs. He worried I'd get stuck on the toilet, fall in the shower, or take a tumble down the stairs. My legs were still shaky; I could walk okay if I consciously locked my knees, but one wrong step sent me stumbling. If I squatted down I couldn't get back up, and I refused to promise I'd stay away from the stairs.

I was torn about having Chris home. I hadn't been alone in my own home in over a week, and I desperately needed solitude to process the overload of thoughts and emotions swirling in my brain. Yet I was terrified of sorting through that mess, and I didn't really trust myself to be alone either. I was the lowest I'd ever been. I'd never dealt with anything so serious before, and my behavior was erratic; I had no idea what I was doing, what I was capable of. Having Chris around was as big of a crutch as my cane, and I needed both to keep moving through my haze.

Monday morning inevitably came. Chris and I lounged in bed on yet another mockingly gorgeous day; everyone kept saying it was the most beautiful July they could remember. Neither of us wanted to get out of bed and face reality. We'd affectionately dubbed our bed "The Bed," for it was a safe haven, a place where we felt secure, the only place where we could curl up and waste the day and get lost in our thoughts. It was also tremendously comfortable.

I was replaying Avery's death in my mind, like I did every morning, when the funeral home called. Chris and I looked at the caller ID; neither of us had the stomach to answer. We vaguely heard a woman leaving a message on the machine in the kitchen.

"What a nice way to start the day," I sighed.

We stayed in bed a bit longer, but the curiosity over our daughter's remains coaxed us out of our room.

The woman on the machine had a small, mousy voice; she sounded sweet and sympathetic. She called to let us know that Avery's body was at the funeral home and was being shipped to the company's crematorium. The remains would be back in a week or so. She wanted us to call her back.

"You can do it," I said, shaking my head and chewing an English muffin doused in raspberry jam. "I can't talk to her."

"Whatever," Chris replied, picking up the phone, a tinge of frustration breaking through his voice. He was getting tired of my helplessness.

I listened carefully as Chris said a series of "thank you"s. The funeral home lady was no doubt telling him how sorry she was, something we were getting used to, and Chris was truly gracious in his thanks. As I watched my husband, I admired his ability to talk about our tragedy; he was such a people person, so much better at accepting condolences and tackling issues head-on. I, on the other hand, was tired of all the compassion. I wanted to crawl into The Bed, pull the covers over my head, and disappear.

Chris returned the phone to its cradle. "We have to get something to put her in," he stated matter-of-factly.

My blood boiled as I stared in disbelief. "What do you mean, we have to get something to put her in? Isn't that their job? Don't they have urns? What the hell are we paying them for?"

"The ones they have there are all really big, and she said there won't be a lot of ashes since Avery is so small," he explained. "She said we can probably pick something up at Hobby Lobby and just drop it off for them. They'll seal it when they get Avery back from the crematorium."

My bloodshot eyes drilled a hole in my husband. Was I really being told that I needed to go choose my daughter's eternal resting place at Hobby Lobby?

"We can go after your doctor's appointment," Chris suggested.

My doctor's appointment. I'd forgotten about that. My doctor was adamant she wanted to see me Monday, no doubt to make sure I was still alive. I wondered if they were worried about a lawsuit. The thought had crossed my mind—but what were they guilty of? They had provided the standard care for a normal pregnancy, which is what I had. There was no indication that anything was out of the ordinary, and I never expressed any major concerns. Based on the data, Avery was a normal baby girl. Somehow we all let her slip through the cracks, and if we started pointing fingers, they would certainly land right back on me. As much as I wished I could pass the blame, my doctors had not been negligent.

My doctor had scheduled the appointment during her lunch hour, no doubt to save me the pain of having to see any happy pregnant women in the waiting room. The staff looked at me with sorrow as I was spared wait time and quickly rushed to an exam room. I longed for the day when people would look at me like a person again instead of a victim.

The doctor entered the room in record time, a thin purple book attached to her clipboard. We chatted about how I was feeling physically before she launched into a list of depression questions to once again evaluate my level of suicidal tendencies. Once she was satisfied that I planned on living to see another day, she handed me the purple book, a book about coping with loss. She also explained she was looking for a weighted teddy bear for me. Evidently holding something of similar weight to the baby was supposed to be a great coping mechanism. I appreciated her thoughtfulness, but I wasn't looking for a book or a bear. All I wanted was a logical, medical explanation for what happened to Avery.

Chris was braver than me.

"So do we have any idea how this happened?" he asked, walking a fine line between anger and curiosity. "I mean, do you think it could have been prevented? And how do we keep it from happening again?"

The doctor gathered her thoughts for a moment. She explained that stillbirths are hard to prevent, mostly because it's hard to tell for sure what causes them. "We don't have the autopsy results back yet," she continued. "And sometimes even that doesn't tell us anything for sure."

While it was pretty obvious to me that the umbilical cord had played a major part in Avery's demise, until we had the autopsy results and all of my blood work there was always the possibility that something else could have killed her, something that could happen again.

I didn't think I could have another baby if there was any chance it would end in stillbirth.

I heard Chris ask how long we had to wait to start trying again. I desperately wanted another baby, but couldn't imagine going through it all again. The waiting, the uncertainty. It was too much.

"I'd like you to wait at least three periods," she answered. "That would make me comfortable. And we will do everything possible to make sure this doesn't happen again. You'll be treated as high-risk, so the third trimester you'll come in twice a week for ultrasounds and non-stress tests."

Why couldn't you have done that with Avery, I thought.

"Can you guarantee it won't happen again?" Chris asked. I felt like he was interviewing her, trying to decide if we wanted to keep her as our doctor if there was a next time.

"Well, we can't have her hooked up to a machine twenty-four hours a day," she replied, pointing at me. "Plus, I don't think you'd want that. But we will do everything we can."

I knew she was joking, but I thought seriously about being hooked up to a machine for nine months, unable to leave the house but constantly knowing the status of my unborn child. I would do it in a heartbeat if it meant I would be guaranteed a healthy, living baby.

The conversation shifted to my legs. She didn't seem overly concerned, but I was terrified that something was seriously wrong. It had been five days; my legs were weak and had shown little improvement. I thought of the hobbies I loved—skiing, tennis, running. I feared I would never do any of them again. I had not only lost my daughter, I had lost everything else I loved, too. It sickened me to be such an invalid.

The doctor told me to be patient, that it would take time, that I needed to start by getting out of the house and walking to build up my muscles. If I didn't want to walk, she could send me to physical therapy.

I laughed out loud as I imagined myself walking around our neighborhood, pushing an empty stroller. I could put my weighted teddy bear in it for extra effect. Or maybe, once Avery's ashes were back, I could push the urn around. The neighbors would love that. Then I pictured my legs giving out, my body slapping the pavement like a falling tree. *Tim-ber!* We had a very quiet neighborhood; I could be stuck in the street for hours, waiting for someone to help me up.

Walking was going to be dangerous. Maybe I needed to get one of those LifeAlert bracelets I'd seen on TV.

My doctor gave me a big hug and her cell phone number, and told me she'd see me again for my six-week checkup. We were escorted out the back door; the after-lunch appointments would be in the waiting room by now, and she didn't want me to see them. Or maybe she didn't want them to see me. I was probably bad for business.

We rolled down the windows of my Acadia, the "family" vehicle we'd purchased three months before Avery's due date, opened the sunroof, and drove to Hobby Lobby, desperately hoping the gorgeous weather would counteract the darkness we felt inside.

*****

I can't begin to tell you how hard it is to pick a container in which to put your child.

The store had dozens of options, but nothing seemed quite right. I was furious to be doing it in the first place. We were paying good money for the funeral home to take care of our daughter's remains; couldn't they find something to put her in? I sifted through zebra-print ceramics, gothic urns straight from Dracula's castle, Asian-inspired boxes. Nothing seemed right for my baby girl.

I was about to give up when I saw a glint of silver out of

the corner of my eye. A simple urn was tucked away behind the flashier merchandise, the only one like it in the store. It was round, small, silver, and simple. An elegant cross graced its lid; I ran my fingers over the embossing, lost in thought.

"Do you think it will rust?" I turned to Chris. The last thing I wanted was to have my daughter's tomb start falling apart after a few years.

"I doubt it," he replied, examining the urn. "It says it's stainless. It should last a while."

"Then this is it," I said definitively. It was only $15, but it was beautiful—elegant and quiet, just like Avery. I said a little prayer to her, hoping she would like her new home.

We stopped at the funeral home on the way back to our house. I made Chris go in alone and drop off the urn, partly because I couldn't walk very well but mostly because I didn't want to go inside. Avery's body wasn't there anymore, it had been shipped north to the crematorium, but the building still held other people's remains. I'd felt enough death.

We returned home to find a delivery van in our driveway and an old man standing on our porch. We instantly recognized him, as it was his third trip to our house; there were only so many flower shops in the area.

"Got another delivery for ya," the gentleman said, handing me a striking bouquet of pink roses in a small, transparent green block vase. The arrangement reminded me of our wedding flowers. Next he handed me a large pink envelope.

"Thanks," I said, taking the flowers and card. It was by far the most beautiful arrangement we had received, the most full of life, and the first to come with an actual card. The others simply contained a few generic words of sympathy on a florist's note.

I opened the envelope and instantly felt a wrench in my heart. The flowers were from my high school yearbook class, and, though they were on summer break, many of my twenty-two students had individually typed me a message. My yearbook editor had collected them and placed them in the card. I wept as I read their kind, poignant words; they were teenagers, naturally self-centered and oblivious, and, while they probably had no concept of the magnitude of what had happened to me, they had taken the time to try.

> *I'm very sorry to hear about your sad news. She will be missed beyond measure, but the love you shared with her is immortal. My deepest sympathy goes out to you and your family.*
>
> *I was so sorry to hear what happened. My prayers are with you, and I wish you and your husband the best.*
>
> *We love you, Mrs. Chandler.*
>
> *I can't even begin to imagine what you guys are feeling. I'm very sorry to hear about the loss of your sweet Avery. God will take care of her and she will be watching over you guys from above. Know many people care about you guys and you will be amazing parents!*
>
> *I wish you all the love in the world.*

These kids had been with me through my entire pregnancy, and their thoughtfulness hit me hard. These students, mostly girls, shared my excitement when I discovered at twenty weeks that my baby was a girl. They convinced me to waste half a class period while they guessed the name we'd chosen. They oohed and ahhed at every ultrasound picture and helped me choose a middle name. They threw me a surprise baby shower at the end of the school year. They bought Avery a swing and a bib that said, "If you think I'm cute, you should see my mom." They offered to babysit. They watched Avery grow inside of me, and they would never get to meet her.

It wasn't fair.

I did my best to dry my tears as I made a turkey sandwich. I'd listened to my doctor and avoided lunchmeat during my pregnancy; now all I wanted to eat was turkey sandwiches.

"That was nice of them," Chris remarked, picking up the card.

I nodded, choking down a bite of food. My throat was dry and my stomach uneasy.

I slowly got up from the table, using it as leverage to get to my feet. "I think I'm going to read in bed." I smiled at Chris, throwing the rest of my sandwich in the trash. "I'm tired."

"That's fine." Chris looked at me, trying to read my emotions. "I need to do some work this afternoon anyway."

I was jealous that Chris had work to do, that he had something else to think about. Though I didn't want to admit it, life was going on without me, without Avery. There was a whole world out there just chugging along as usual, with business deals and lunch meetings and coffee breaks and kids' soccer games. First dates and weddings, birthdays and new babies. Just because I was stuck in a perpetual state of misery didn't mean everyone else was.

I washed my face and stared hard at the mirror. I looked the same, but everything had changed. My life would never go back to the way it was. I thought of the fluidity of life, of how we're supposed to change and grow and become better, stronger people. But I was unprepared to change so quickly, so violently, and I had no idea how to move forward.

I didn't want to move forward.

I crawled into bed with the book from my doctor, hoping to find answers, to uncover the reason why God had decided to take my baby away. After two brief pages I closed the book, placed it on the nightstand, and soaked my pillow with tears.

*****

Desperate to feel better, I turned to the stack of pamphlets the hospital had sent home. I picked up the first one, a purple paper folded in three titled "The Five Stages of Grief." I flipped through it, learning I would start with Denial and move through Anger, Bargaining, and Depression before I finally found Acceptance. I was fairly certain I was past Denial, so I read through the next three stages, looking for a time frame for how long I could expect to be stuck in each one. Would I feel this way for weeks? Months? Years?

The only thing I found was the statement, "Everyone's grief is different."

No shit.

I grabbed a pink one called "Coping with Your Loss." It told me that loss often leaves the survivor feeling sad and hopeless.

No shit.

I read "A Mother's Guide to Loss." It suggested I purchase a notebook and begin writing down my feelings.

Feelings. I chuckled at the thought. I didn't have any damn feelings. I was completely numb.

To humor myself, I grabbed a pen and paper and started writing.

HOW I FEEL:
Bad
Really Bad
Really, Really Bad
Really, Really, Really Bad

What a fucking joke, I thought, tossing the paper in the garbage.

I spent the next few days in isolation, talking as little as possible. A month's worth of food had arrived at our house, so that negated any need to go to the grocery store. We contemplated using the boat, but I needed to stay out of the water for six weeks to avoid infection, so we opted to stay on dry land. Chris busied himself with work while I drifted around the house avoiding the rest of the world. I refused to answer the phone and kept my distance from the front door. The plants and floral arrangements had come to a halt, but more cards trickled in as the news of Avery's death passed down the wire. I placed the cards in the mountainous pile and vowed to read them once I had the house to myself.

Each morning I gimped to the mailbox with my cane, acting like a fugitive, first making sure no neighbors were outside. I didn't want to see anyone; I didn't want my neighbors giving sympathetic looks or asking questions I couldn't answer. I worried those who hadn't heard the news would ask how my baby was, since it was obvious I was no longer pregnant. And I didn't need anyone else telling me how Cousin Sally's aunt's sister's daughter had lost a child or how my daughter was in "a better place." I wanted to be a hermit, to hide from a world that didn't understand my pain.

Chris was a wonderful husband, keeping his distance yet offering support, but I was still alone in my grief. I knew he had to blame me for Avery's death—I was the one who let her die. The grief pamphlets shouted, "It's not your fault," but it was my fault. Avery was my responsibility, and I had failed my daughter. In doing that, I had failed my husband. Every hour I sank deeper into my dark place, torturing myself for failing to notice the signs of Avery's slow demise and livid with my body for not doing its job.

The only thing that kept me sane was educating myself, attempting to discover what had happened to my baby. I spent hours each day searching the Internet for every scrap of information on stillbirth and cord accidents. Knowledge was power, and, since I was completely powerless, it was the only way I could feel some semblance of control. But the more I learned, the angrier I became.

One study hypothesized that most stillbirths occurred at night. I shivered as I recalled getting up to pee two nights before my water broke. I sat on the toilet, half asleep, and felt Avery's tiny foot wedged hard against my left rib, pushing, harder and harder, until I couldn't breathe. I tried to push her foot down but she pressed harder, determined to get my attention. Was she dying then? Is that what she was trying to tell me? Was she asking for my help? She needed me, and I went back to bed, annoyed that she was making me uncomfortable.

I printed off statistics to show Chris, thrusting the loose papers in his face with disgust. Different sites cited different numbers, since apparently there is no national database for recording stillbirths. One out of every 100 pregnancies end in stillbirth, one out of every 120, one out of every 160—the exact numbers didn't matter to me, what mattered was that it was so common. I couldn't believe that there were over 30,000 in the U.S. every year, yet I hadn't read about stillbirth in any of my pregnancy books. While I found solace that there were other women like me, it also made me furious.

I rambled off more information to my husband.

"Fifteen to twenty percent of stillborn babies have one or more birth defects. Placental problems, primarily placental abruption, cause twenty-five percent of stillbirths. Forty percent of stillborn babies have poor growth. Ten percent of stillbirths are linked to health problems in the mother, like high blood pressure and diabetes. Smokers are more apt to have stillbirths. Infections cause ten to twenty-five percent of stillbirths. African American women, obese women, and women over thirty-five are more likely to have a stillbirth. Fifty percent of stillbirths have no listed cause. Umbilical cord accidents account for two to four percent of all stillbirths. Most stillbirths occur around thirty-six weeks."

Avery was just past that.

I trembled as I slammed the papers on the kitchen counter. I couldn't fathom how something so terrible was so prevalent in a civilized society. How, with all the technology available today, were babies still dying? And how, with as many as one out of every hundred pregnancies ending this way, was no one talking about it? If it happened to Angelina or Mrs. Tom Cruise or some other celebrity, the lead story at every news outlet would be "Stillbirth—The Silent Terror." People would be devastated, demanding doctors do more to save these poor, helpless babies. We'd hear about it over and over again for weeks, even months, clogging up Facebook pages and Twitter feeds, until a national holiday was declared and Congress enacted a bill mandating twenty-four-hour monitoring for all pregnant women.

But it didn't happen to someone famous; it happened to me, an ordinary high school teacher in West Michigan. I wasn't important enough, Avery wasn't important enough, for the rest of the world to care. At that moment I vowed to become a stillbirth vigilante, to scream from the rooftops that we weren't going to suffer in silence. I was going to change the world in the name of my daughter, in the name of all of those babies whose eyes would never see the light of day.

And then I thought of my sweet Avery, of her lifeless body as I held her in my arms, of those bow lips, redder than the reddest rose. I thought of that delicate body and those chubby cheeks, lying still in a box at a crematorium, waiting to be placed in an oven and turned to dust.

My anger twisted to sadness. I crawled back in bed and sobbed, hopeless and alone.

CHAPTER THIRTEEN

Chris played softball on Wednesday nights. It was the one-week anniversary of Avery's birth/death, and I couldn't believe he was actually going to play.

"Are you coming with me?" Chris looked serious, pulling his blue We Don't Slide t-shirt over his head. I noticed that his bald spot had grown a little in the past week. "You don't have to, but I'd feel better if you came."

Avery and I had been fixtures at Wednesday night softball. We sat in the dusty dugout and kept score, cheering on his co-ed rec league team as my belly grew. After the games we went to an Irish pub for drinks and dinner. I would sip a tall glass of Sprite and devour a plate of greasy onion rings while the rest of the team drank beer.

I looked at myself, pathetic in the same frayed pink flannel pants and hooded Michigan State sweatshirt I'd worn since returning from the hospital, despite the fact that the temperature outside was well over eighty degrees.

"I don't have anything to wear," I grumbled. It wasn't completely untrue; none of my pre-pregnancy clothes fit me, and wearing maternity clothes just seemed weird.

Chris studied my face carefully. "If you don't want to come, you don't have to, but I think it would be good for you to get out of the house."

I was mad at him for suggesting it, but I knew he was right. I was too satisfied with my solitude. I needed to get out, to have an actual conversation, to walk amongst living, breathing human beings. But seclusion was comfortable; it was easy. Going out in public was not. These people were our friends; most had visited us, yet the thought of seeing them made me squirm. I didn't know what to say, and I didn't know how they would react. I was a walking fun-wrecker; I made people feel bad and think sad thoughts. I felt everyone would be better off if they didn't have to see me, the walking reminder of death.

It would have been easy to tell Chris no, to spend the evening alone with the Internet or in the safety of The Bed. It had only been a week since I had given birth to Avery—no one could blame me for craving privacy. But I had a war brewing inside. I knew the more I avoided social interaction the more withdrawn I would inevitably become. And I could sense there was a real possibility I could put myself so far in a dark corner it would be impossible to walk in the sunlight again.

"Fine," I huffed, turning to my closet. "I'll go."

I plucked a sherbet orange eyelet skirt from its hanger. It wasn't a maternity skirt, but it had a drawstring waist. I struggled a bit pulling it over my widened hips, but other than that it fit. I settled on a white maternity t-shirt with a jean jacket to complete the ensemble.

I dabbed concealer under my eyes in a futile attempt to hide the dark circles, then added mascara and bronzer, hoping to look healthy and alive.

"You look fine," Chris said, anxious to leave. I really did look fine, considering what I'd been through, but I still felt terrible. I was awkward, horribly uncomfortable in my own skin, and it was going to take more than makeup and a wardrobe change to fix that.

It was a nine p.m. game, and it was nearly dark when we arrived at the ball fields. As we walked toward the dugout, I held tight to Chris's hand like a child on her first day of school. He wouldn't let me sit in the bleachers, since that involved climbing stairs and I'd refused to bring my cane. I started to protest but quickly stopped when I realized I'd have the opportunity to linger unseen in the shadows. As his teammates arrived, they looked surprised to see me sitting on the bench, then offered hugs and asked how I was doing. With every embrace I fought back tears; I loved that people cared, but I wished they didn't have to care.

For the first time in a week Chris had a genuine smile on his face, laughing and joking with his friends, tossing the ball around the field and cheering on his teammates. I envied his laughter, yet I was glad I was there to witness him letting go for a short time and being himself, the wonderful man I had fallen in love with years before.

I wondered if that would ever happen to me.

Nonetheless, a melancholy cloud hung over the game, and everyone was a little quieter than usual. Avery was known as Chris's good luck charm, as the only two games they had lost that season were when Avery and I couldn't attend.

This was the final game of the season, and they won in grand fashion. I looked up at the stars splashed across the eastern sky and saw one burning brighter than the rest, begging to be noticed. At that moment I knew the littlest angel, my angel, was watching over us from above, outshining all the others, making sure her daddy won this game, too.

*****

Friday night we made plans to have dinner with our friends Jim and Carol. Rather, Chris made plans to have dinner with Jim and Carol.

"What do you mean we're going to dinner?" I glared at my husband. I was pissed.

Chris lifted his hands in exasperation. "It's just dinner. They asked, and it's good for us to get out. It's just an hour or two."

I dreaded the thought of leaving my sanctuary again, of having to smile and chat and pretend that the world wasn't crumbling around me.

And I didn't have anything to wear.

"Fine. But don't expect me to have fun."

We walked into Don Pablo's Mexican restaurant late due to a few wardrobe malfunctions on my part. It was hot outside, but I settled on a jean jacket over a black tee in a semi-successful attempt to hide my muffin top. Chris told me I was being too hard on myself, that it hadn't even been two weeks since I'd had a baby. In my mind, since I didn't physically *have* the baby, I didn't have a legitimate excuse for the extra rolls.

As we weaved through the crowd toward our table, I prayed not to see anyone who recognized me, partly because I wasn't in the mood for awkward condolences, but mostly because I didn't want to have to tell my story all over again to someone who hadn't heard. Thankfully I hadn't been put in that situation yet (because I never left the house), and I wasn't quite sure what to say or how to react. I was walking on eggshells with myself, but I knew somewhere deep inside was a landmine waiting to explode.

It also felt strange that I was out and about so soon, dining with friends and having a "good time." What kind of monster would people think I was?

Jim and Carol, two truly wonderful people, were sipping cocktails at the table when we sat down. I'd already seen them twice—they stopped by our house the day I returned from the hospital, and I had seen them again at the softball game—so there was no need for the customary "I'm sorry"s or "how are you"s. They told me I looked great and that was that. Then we talked about other things, for the night was about bringing us back from the land of the lost, about showing us we were still human beings capable and deserving of fun.

I hesitantly ordered a Corona with lime. I hadn't had a drink in nine months, and I wasn't sure what alcohol was going to do to me. The last thing I needed was to add to my depression, to burst into tears in the middle of a crowded restaurant or lock myself in a bathroom stall. But the instant the cold beer touched my lips, it tasted divine.

My second beer tasted pretty good, too.

And my third.

Dinner went by quickly, and our friends insisted we head over to the patio at the Waterfront, a local bar overlooking the lake. Chris glanced sideways at me for an answer, and I responded with a tipsy shrug. I couldn't believe it, but I was almost enjoying myself.

As we sipped our drinks in the evening breeze and watched a cotton-candy sunset disappear over the glassy lake, I decided I was going to be drunk by night's end, and I refused to feel guilty about it. For the first time in weeks, I began to relax, if only for a moment. I caught myself smiling without rehearsing it first, laughing without forcing it. Instead of talking about dead babies, I danced in my chair and sang Journey's greatest hits along with the band. I was amazed at how well I could breathe.

Chris grabbed my hand as the band started our song, "Don't Stop Believing," and I leaned over and gave him a kiss.

"Are you having fun?" he whispered in my ear.

I flashed him a goofy smile and nodded. "Yes," I laughed. "I'm having fun."

I was officially drunk.

And it felt really, really good.

My grief literature warned that drinking was the last thing a grieving person should do. But somehow, in that moment, surrounded by cold drinks and good friends, I was able to let go of my pain for a few hours. I felt a little more alive, a little more normal. I felt a little more like me, whoever that person now was.

CHAPTER FOURTEEN

We brought Avery home on a Wednesday, exactly two weeks after the day of her birth. My husband returned to the office that week, leaving me to roam the house in peace. I hadn't left since our Friday night on the town, and when I received the call that Avery's remains would be ready Wednesday morning I immediately called Chris at work, telling him I didn't have the stomach to get her by myself.

"That's fine," he replied. I was surprised by his answer; I'd expected him to be annoyed by my dependency. "I'll come home for lunch, and we can get her together."

For the two weeks leading up to that day, I told myself over and over that I would feel better once Avery was home. Once I was able to put her in her own room, I would have some semblance of closure. Once she was back where she belonged, I would finally be at peace. I put a lot of pressure on that day, and I half expected to feel some sort of cathartic release that would magically take me back to the person I used to be, the person I so desperately wanted to be again.

I was terrified I would be disappointed.

My body trembled as we pulled into the parking lot of the funeral home. Butterflies danced in my stomach, and I started to feel lightheaded. My palms were slimy with sweat.

"Are you okay?" Chris asked, watching me wring my hands.

"I think so," I answered. "I'm just really nervous. I don't know why." I felt the same as I had when I first peed on that stick nine and a half months earlier, anxious and scared and excited, yet uncertain about the future.

We walked into the stately brick building holding hands, an unbreakable unit on a mission to complete our family. A tall man who looked exactly like he worked in a funeral home greeted us. He was eerily cheery for someone who spent his days with the dead, and he directed us to the woman who had our daughter.

"Hello," the young woman sang sweetly.

I recognized her voice from the answering machine. She looked just as sweet as she sounded—young, vibrant, and full of life.

"You must be the Chandlers. I'm so sorry for your loss. We have your daughter back here."

We followed her into the employee area, where she filled out an invoice. Chris handed over his credit card. It seemed strange that we had to pay to get our daughter back, but I suppose business is business.

"Here is this." She smiled, picking up the small container holding Avery.

I held my breath as she gently placed the urn in my outstretched hands. I smiled as she let go, pleasantly surprised by the weight. We were told there would be very few ashes for such a small child, so I'd expected Avery to be much lighter. I was strangely comforted that I could still feel her weight in my arms, even if it was much less than it had been two weeks before.

"And here is your cremation certificate," she explained, handing me an envelope. "If you ever decide to have her buried, you'll need this."

It stung that we didn't have a birth certificate to confirm our daughter's existence, yet we had a cremation certificate. Why would we need that for a person who didn't exist? I stared at the paper in my hands, a small white envelope with two small words typed in black.

Avery Chandler.

It was the first time I had seen her full name in print, and it made me happy. It was a good name, a pretty name, and it belonged to my daughter. A real person had that name; Avery Chandler was a bona fide human being.

We said our thank-yous and goodbyes, and we were finally able to take our sweet girl home.

As Chris started the car, I stared dumbly down at the urn sitting on my lap.

"Well?" he asked, giving me a smile. "Do you feel better?"

I gave a nervous, childish grin and turned back to the urn. Slowly, I took it in my hands and shook it lightly, then with more force. I could feel the contents of the container shift with every shake. I held the urn up to my ear and shook it again, listening to soft whooshing that was my daughter. It was almost like hearing her heartbeat.

Almost.

"She's in there," I said, beaming.

"You're a dork," Chris laughed, grabbing my hand and giving it a playful squeeze.

I looked like a crazy woman, I'm sure, shaking the ashes of my dead daughter with glee. Maybe I *was* crazy, but it felt so good to have her back. She wasn't the same Avery I held in my arms at the hospital, yet she was. She was my daughter, and a weight was lifted off my shoulders now that I was finally taking her home where she belonged, to spend eternity with her family.

After a quick lunch Chris went back to work, leaving me alone with Avery. I watched his car pull away and stared curiously at the urn, half expecting some ectoplasmic apparition of my baby to come swirling out of the container.

"Are you in there, sweet girl?" I whispered, softly shaking the urn. "Can you hear me?"

Silence.

I watched the container a little longer. I'm not exactly sure what I expected to happen upon Avery's arrival home, but no magic hung in the air. I didn't hear the supernatural mew of a newborn baby (although the grief brochures said that could happen), and there was no drastic sign that anything in my life had changed. My daughter was still dead. Yet somehow, inexplicably, I felt calmer. The intense anxiety that had plagued me for two weeks disappeared, and I could actually think straight. My life wasn't perfect, but it was more right than it had been with Avery missing from my home.

I picked up my daughter and headed to the couch. Chris had placed a framed photo of Avery on the mantle, which was a point of contention between us. Whenever we expected a friend to visit or the cleaning people to come I took it down, but by the time they arrived it would be back up again. I couldn't stand to watch people's eyes dart around the room, trying to find something to look at other than my daughter's picture.

"It makes people uncomfortable," I told Chris. "It grosses people out. They don't want to see our dead baby."

"I don't care," Chris replied. "It's my daughter. If they don't like it, they can leave."

Now I stared at the picture and smiled, holding the urn securely in my arms in an awkward embrace.

"Welcome home, baby girl," I whispered. "Welcome home."

We spent the afternoon together, mother and child, watching TV.

It took me hours to muster the courage to take Avery upstairs to her room. I'd avoided the nursery since my return from the hospital, and I probably could have continued to avoid it if I really wanted to. But I was Avery's mother, and it was my job to put her where she belonged.

I gingerly climbed the stairs, one hand on the banister, the other cradling my daughter. I stopped outside the maple door, which, as far as I knew, had been closed since Avery's birthday. I took a deep breath and turned the knob, opening a portal to a world I had left behind.

The room was stuffy and smelled of all things baby, powders and lotions and freshly washed clothes. It was late afternoon, and the warm July sunshine poured through the windows, the shadows of our ancient trees dancing on the walls. I glanced at the curtains I had fallen in love with for the room, gauzy white cotton covered in tiny embroidered pink roses. I laughed as I watched the sunlight surge through. What a stupid choice for a baby's room; they did a piss-poor job of blocking the light. Avery never would have slept.

The mint green walls were still bright and cheery—celery was the paint color—a perfect complement to the maple crib and changing table we'd thoroughly debated at Babies 'R Us. The cabinets were stocked with the tiniest diapers, the drawers filled with fluffy blankets and burpcloths covered in purple butterflies and pink polka dots.

I felt a lump in my throat and a pang of guilt as I glanced at the empty crib dressed in its white and red ladybug sheets. My brother and his wife had bought Avery's bedding, a pink-and-green gingham set with a ladybug theme. I loved that bedding; it reminded me of my own room as a child. The set wasn't cheap, and I felt terrible that they'd wasted all that money on something that might not ever be used.

I walked over to the crib and placed Avery inside, like I was putting my newborn baby down for her first nap.

"Well, this is your room, sweetie pie," I said. "Not exactly how I envisioned putting you in your crib for the first time, but this will have to do."

I couldn't help but wonder if Avery's death was my destiny, Chris's destiny, or our destiny. If I had married a different man, would my first child still have died? If Chris had married a different woman, would he have lost his firstborn? Or was it something God had reserved just for us—a storm we were meant to weather together, to teach us some sort of sick lesson about life.

I looked around the room at all of the baby stuff, all of the *girl* baby stuff, from the fluffy pink stuffed animals and pastel blankets to the pink and purple pacifiers. As nervous as I had been about becoming a mother, we were truly ready for her to come into our lives. The love and caring with which her room had been put together reinforced that.

I plodded over to a shelf and picked up a small brown teddy bear dressed in a red t-shirt that said HUGS FROM AVERY. My mom gave the bears away at one of my baby showers, a scant two weeks before Avery's delivery. At my mother's insistence, everyone had happily rubbed my pregnant belly with the bears for good luck. I wondered if the attendees had quietly disposed of their bears when they heard of Avery's death.

I gave the bear a quick squeeze and placed it back on the shelf.

I was proud of my composure on my first visit to the nursery. It wasn't so bad being there, especially since I had Avery with me. I smiled as I looked at my daughter again, finally home in her crib where she belonged.

I walked to the closet door and opened the double doors, something I hadn't anticipated doing. Inside, arranged by size and hanging on tiny pink and green plastic hangers, were dozens of outfits, most of them pink, all of them tiny and adorable. I ran my hand across the fabrics, stopping on my favorites. There was the first thing I ever bought for Avery, the tiny purple-and-white flowered dress I bought at Old Navy the day I found out we were having a girl. I touched the yellow polo dress with matching bloomers from my best friend Nicky, the beautiful white handmade gown from my mom's friend Carole, and a twelve-month-sized red, white, and blue July Fourth outfit I'd picked up three days before my water broke. My body physically ached from their touch; sorrow rushed through my veins. I imagined the Avery I had seen two weeks ago wearing those clothes, but this time alive.

She would have been so beautiful.

Life was not fair. I should be choosing Avery's outfit for the day, not deciding where to keep her ashes.

At some point I started to cry. I found myself on the floor, out of control and gasping for air, fighting the convulsions of grief.

"Why, why, why, why?" I heard myself sob, begging for answers from a silent deity. I pounded my clenched fists against the floor, against the wall, until my knuckles began to crack and bleed. "It's not fair," I howled like a wounded animal, screaming at the ceiling fan. "It's just not fair. How could you take her away? Why did you take my baby away?"

I crawled to the crib and grabbed Avery, hugging her close to my chest, rocking her back and forth on the floor.

"I'm so sorry," I wept, tears splashing on the roof of her home. I ran my fingers over the cross, wiping away the wetness. "I'm sorry I couldn't save you, Avery. I'm sorry I didn't know. I'm so sorry, baby girl. I'm so sorry..."

It had been two weeks since her death, and I told myself things were getting better, that I wasn't quite as depressed and everything was going to be fine. Friends and family constantly told me Avery's death was not my fault, and I had almost convinced myself that was true. But at that moment, as I lay on the floor of my only child's room soaked in my own tears, I knew I was lying to myself. I was lost in a sinister world, a place where the death of my daughter weighed on me more than anyone knew. The guilt was eating my soul, the shame quietly devouring my mind. I was suffocating, silently driving myself insane obsessing over questions that would never be answered.

I needed to know why God took Avery away from me. Someone had to explain to me why I wasn't able to save the life I had nurtured and loved every day for almost thirty-eight weeks. I needed to hear why, of the thousands of babies born every day, it was my sweet daughter who became an angel, leaving my family to suffer, leaving me to somehow fill the aching void she left behind.

"It's not fair," I mumbled, carelessly wiping snot on the sleeve of my sweatshirt. "It's not fucking fair. How am I supposed to do this? What am I supposed to do?"

I closed my eyes and waited for an answer.

There was nothing but silence.

My body quivered with the remnants of my breakdown; my abdominal muscles ached from the force of my sobs. My watery red eyes gazed around the room, so cheerful, so welcoming, so perfect for a happy little girl to grow up in. I saw an infant Avery crawling on the soft cream carpeting, a giggling toddler Avery sitting in the miniature white rocking chair with her stuffed green frog, a little girl Avery singing songs and playing with her dolls and staring out the big windows at the birds chirping in the tall trees. Memories of my daughter were everywhere in that room, as was the ghost of the child she would never become.

If I had anything left in my body I would have cried some more, but that well was dry.

I focused on the urn, pressed tightly to my chest in a desperate hug. Chris and I had decided we would place Avery on one of the wall shelves in her nursery, nestled between two cuddly teddy bears, where she could sleep soundly in the room created just for her.

Using the toy chest for support, I pushed my drained body to its feet. I traveled slowly to the shelves, clutching Avery with both hands. I gently kissed the top of the urn and hesitantly placed her on the shelf.

"I love you, baby girl," I whispered, resting my fingers against the cold steel holding the ashes. "I love you so much."

With an aching heart, I gave my daughter one last kiss and closed the door.

CHAPTER FIFTEEN

The first day I left the house by myself was July 23.

I had grown gloriously comfortable in my miserable solitude. Family and the closest friends lived at least two or more hours away, so each day when Chris left for work I found myself truly alone. On good days I ventured outside to cut a bouquet of gladioli from my flower garden or trim my neglected roses, stealthily dodging my neighbors. But most days I stayed indoors.

I'd received a teddy bear and a fleece rainbow-covered blanket from my doctor—"for brighter days"—and I spent hours wandering aimlessly through the halls of my home wrapped in rainbows, alternately hugging a teddy bear and an urn.

Racked with guilt, I always ended up blaming myself. It was my fault Avery died. It was my fault I was sad. It was my fault I couldn't let Avery go. It was my fault I couldn't leave the house. It was my fault I was still fat. It was my fault my life was terrible.

I hated myself. I hated what my life had become.

I rotated between sleeping, crying, browsing the Internet for information on stillbirth, feeling sorry for myself, and expecting answers regarding Avery's death to magically appear. Chris had dutifully handled the phone calls during the first week; now I simply didn't answer the phone if it rang. On the rare occasions I actually talked to people the conversation was painfully awkward. People didn't know how to talk about Avery; I didn't know how to talk about Avery. I made people uncomfortable, so avoidance was my best option. I started treating my daughter like a dirty little secret, because that was the easiest thing for me to do.

The only person I could really talk to was Chris. I spent my days in silence, talking in my head. But when he came home at night my thoughts and feelings were instantly purged all over his dinner plate. I had to talk to somebody, and he was Avery's father, after all. He was the only person I knew whose pain could come close to my own.

Chris listened carefully, but with each day that passed I could tell he was growing weary of my desperation. He was no longer trapped inside those four walls, breathing only the nightmare of our loss; his life was moving on.

"You need to stop blaming yourself," he said. "You need to stop feeling so guilty."

I knew he was right. But guilt isn't a feeling that passes with the next sunrise; it's a sensation that lingers. It ebbs and flows, receding one day and then smothering you the next, a tidal wave of epic proportion drowning any attempt at happiness. I truly wanted to let go of my guilt, but I didn't know how.

I eventually stopped talking about Avery. As far as Chris knew my silence meant my grieving was coming to an end. He had no idea how I spent my days, because I conveniently didn't tell him. Dinner was on the table each night, and I smiled and made conversation. I did what a good wife was supposed to do. But I was miserable.

When we brought Avery home, I told myself I would put her in her room where she could rest in peace. Most days, however, I carried her ashes around the house. We'd watch TV and eat lunch together. She'd sit on the sink while I showered; she'd rest on the kitchen counter while I sliced vegetables. It was absurd, but the only time I felt better was when she was near me. Avery and I lived in our own little bubble, untouched by the outside world.

On the day I received an email from Taylor, one of my newspaper photographers, I immediately felt sick. She needed to pick up a camera from my classroom for journalism camp; I was the only one with keys to the camera cabinet. That meant I had to physically leave the house.

I was going to have to see people, to talk to them. I didn't want to do it. I didn't know if I could.

I panicked and stared at the computer screen, contemplating ignoring the message. All I had to do was hit Delete and say I never got it. No one would ever know, and I could stay lost in my hideout. I gently placed my index finger on Delete and stared at the message for five, ten, fifteen minutes. But I couldn't do it. I was lost, depressed, and mildly insane, but I was still a good teacher. I couldn't let one of my students down.

On the morning of July 23, I tried to look my best. I showered, put on makeup, and did my hair in something other than a greasy ponytail. Still full of baby fat, I opted to wear an outfit I knew would fit, the same orange skirt, white tee, and jean jacket I had thrown together for the softball game.

When I turned down the school entrance I saw a dozen or so cars in the staff parking lot. It was summer vacation, but the administration worked year-round, and there were always a handful of overachieving teachers who wanted to get a jump on the school year. I carefully stepped out of my SUV; the last thing I needed was for my legs to give out in the parking lot. Today I was a Navy Seal—my goal was to get in and out quickly, drawing as little attention as possible.

The school entrance sat atop a long podium of stairs. I didn't have my cane, so I ascended them carefully, one by one, holding tightly to the railing with every tedious step. Going up wasn't as tricky as going down would be; I vowed to use the handicap entrance on the side of the building when I left. As I walked, I kept my eyes averted, praying no one saw me as I entered the building. Perhaps someone did, but I made it to my classroom untouched.

When the young woman came for her camera, I did my best to be upbeat, as did she. It was a quick, painless exchange that took less than a minute, and I was anxious to return home to my refuge. As I locked the classroom door, I heard footsteps closing in from behind. I closed my eyes and took a deep breath before I turned, preparing myself for the conversation.

It was the school librarian, a tiny woman in her fifties, one of the kindest people on the planet. If I was going to have to talk to somebody, it might as well be her.

She offered a teary smile, an expression I was too used to seeing. "I'm so sorry about what happened," she said softly, giving me a quick hug.

I returned her smile, wiping away a renegade tear. That was another reason I hated seeing people: they made me feel, which in turn made me cry. "Thank you," I said, fighting to keep it together. I refused to have a breakdown on my first solo flight.

"Are you doing okay?" she inquired, placing a bony hand on my shoulder.

My initial reaction was to say what I felt, which was, "My daughter unexpectedly died on me three weeks ago. How the hell do you think I'm doing?" But after listening to Chris handle dozens of sympathy calls, I'd memorized his script. I opted to steal his lines and demeanor.

"We're as good as can be expected," I sighed, shaking my head in deep thought. "I mean, there's only so much we can do about it. What's done is done." I pushed back a deranged giggle, for I sounded exactly like my husband.

"I was very upset when I heard the news; we all were," she said in her hushed librarian voice. "Now if you need anything, let me know."

And with that, my first unaccompanied encounter with the outside world was over.

I drove home feeling a little lighter, a little more capable. By the time I parked the car in the garage I'd convinced myself it was the perfect day to venture outdoors. It was finally time for me to leave the house and go for that doctor-prescribed walk. I changed into a pair of shorts that were too tight in the ass, but I didn't care. I laced up my shoes and headed out the door before I could change my mind.

The weather was like every other Godforsaken day that July, balmy and clear and gorgeous, and the early afternoon sunshine warmed my sheltered body. It felt good to be outside, but I had to concentrate on every step just to stay on my feet. I strode carefully along the tree-lined streets, determined not to let my knees give out and end up prostrate, screaming for help.

My small neighborhood was peaceful, as most residents were at work. I left my iPod at home and savored the sounds of birds frolicking across the summer sky and the light breeze tickling the big oaks. It was the same neighborhood I had walked hundreds of times before, but it looked completely different. The flowers seemed a little brighter, the smell of fresh-cut grass a little sweeter.

Perhaps it was because I wasn't used to walking so slowly, but I noticed so many little things, the things we tend to overlook in this mess we call life. Those little things actually made me smile, from the shaggy bunny carelessly munching a neighbor's prized hostas to the buzz of a bumblebee whizzing by my head on his way to pollinate the next flower. I was finally reminded that I was still alive and walking this earth, even if my sweet daughter was not.

*****

I decided to go through the sympathy cards on a Tuesday, almost four weeks after that dreadful day. At one point we were receiving at least ten cards a day, but the commiseration had trickled to a halt. I was left with over a hundred unopened cards watching me from the kitchen counter. I wanted to hear the kind words, to see who took the time, but I was terrified of what it would do to me. I was tired of crying, tired of being sad, and completely exhausted from my emotional meltdowns. I'd gone a few days without losing it; I didn't want to start all over again. Yet reading the cards was something I had to do, a sort of catharsis to get me over the next hump of grief.

I grabbed Avery from her room—after all, the cards were for her, too—and settled on the living room floor with my basket of well-wishes.

The first card I read was from one of the secretaries at school. It was a simple card with a white cat on the front. It said *Thinking of You* and contained a brief handwritten message saying she was praying for us.

"See, Heidi, that wasn't so bad," I said. I closed the card and started a "Read" pile.

I slowly opened one envelope after another, reading messages from friends, coworkers, aunts, cousins, family friends, and near strangers. People I hadn't seen in ten, twenty, even thirty years had taken the time to express their sympathy. I went from feeling completely alone to feeling an outpouring of love.

Some of the cards contained Bible verses that were meant to provide comfort, and a few contained prayer cards to let us know entire congregations had us in their prayers. I appreciated others were talking to God for me, but as far as I was concerned, I wasn't on speaking terms with the man upstairs. He had taken the most precious thing I had ever known away from me, and I wasn't talking to Him until he apologized.

After a while I began seeing duplicates; there were only so many fitting sympathy cards on the market that summer. The most common was probably the most appropriate, and before it was all said and done I found myself with seven of them.

I have known you in my dreams, little one, and there you will forever be loved. Saying goodbye to what might have been, the hopes and dreams that grew more real every day, brings an added sadness to the depth of pain.

Wishing you gentle comfort for your sorrow.

The words made me sad, but I kept the drawbridge locked on my moat of tears.

The vast majority let the card do the talking for them and scrawled a simple *Sorry for your loss* or *Our thoughts are with you.* A handful of people wrote personal messages, and it was

obvious from their carefully chosen words they had spent a
significant amount of time searching for the "right" thing to say.
Those were the cards that touched me most.

I was cruising along, absorbing the love and actually feeling
better, not worse, from the flood of compassion. I was halfway
through the stack when I came across a card containing a
handwritten note. It was a large, ugly card with a picture of
wheat grass, a card I guessed was chosen by an older person. As
I unfolded the note, I could tell from the meticulous script that
my speculation was correct.

It was from my great-aunt, my paternal grandfather's sister,
a relative I had only seen a handful of times throughout my life.
My heart broke as I read her words.

*Many years ago (1950), I was in a hospital in Columbus,
Ohio, sobbing because I had miscarried our first child. The
nurses said, "You'll have other children," and they were right—I
had four of them.*

*No one knows why bad things happen to good people through
no fault of their own. Just know that your little girl is safe in God's
keeping and carry on. Better days are ahead.*

I folded the note and placed it back in the card, flattered she
had shared something so personal. Our situations were different,
yet I somehow felt she knew my pain.

Better days are ahead.

They had to be.

I wiped away a tear and plugged on, determined to stay
strong. I read cards from my doctors, cards from the nurses
who had taken care of me during my endless days and nights in
the hospital. A girl I barely knew in high school had found my
address. The more I read the more amazed I became that my
little six-pound fourteen-ounce daughter had touched so many.

As strong as I was, I knew that reading the cards would
eventually turn me into a basket case. The card that finally did
me in was from my cousin, a tough guy who I couldn't believe

actually sent a card. It was a Van Gogh-ish illustration of a starry sky.

The words tore at my soul.

I have this feeling there's one more star up in the sky tonight. And even though it's far away, its brightness and warmth still reach us here to make the night a little less dark.

My tears poured, but I didn't feel them. My heart was numb yet throbbing; I felt so alone yet so loved. Avery was real and she was special. Not just to me, but to others, too, and that validated her existence, her worth. She was somebody, a real person that people cared about and loved and missed, even though they never had a chance to meet her.

My daughter, the shining star, brighter than the rest, watching over us from above.

I just had to believe that was true.

CHAPTER SIXTEEN

My confidence was slowly building and our fridge quickly emptying, so the following day I decided it was time for a trip to the grocery store. I'd spent the morning with Avery next to me on the sofa, reading magazines and watching the women of *The View* bicker about the latest Hot Topic. As I grabbed my purse and headed for the door I said goodbye to my daughter, still sitting quietly on the beige loveseat. She looked so lonely all by herself, at least as lonely as an inanimate object can look, so after a split second of irrational deliberation, I decided to take her with me. I gently placed the urn in the passenger seat and drove to the store.

I held my head high as I walked through the automatic doors of the local megastore everyone shopped at, reminding myself that, although I had frequented the same store while pregnant, no one there knew me and no one knew what happened. My plan was to quietly go about my business and get out as quickly as possible.

I hadn't considered the effect weeks of near isolation would have on my senses, and as I entered the building the fluorescent lights, loud music, and number of people shopping simply overwhelmed me. I stood frozen, a gawking spectator from another planet, feeling conspicuous and alone. A woman walked by and gave me a strange smile; was she one of the nurses who'd taken care of me in the hospital? I looked at the greeter, an older woman I had seen countless times before. I was sure she recognized me. Was she going to ask about my baby?

I sucked in a deep breath and closed my eyes. "You can do this," I whispered. "You have to do this."

I grabbed a shopping cart and reflexively started pushing, doing my best to shake off my paranoia and seem normal while avoiding eye contact. My heart thumped in my chest; I was burning up. Beads of sweat dripped from my forehead, and my dry tongue clung to the roof of my mouth.

I made it through the produce section and was headed toward dairy when I saw her. She was tiny and perfect, sound asleep, wrapped snugly in a pink blanket. She was no more than a month old, perched on top of a cart in a pink-and-brown car seat, much like the one we had for Avery. I stopped in my tracks and stared, fighting back the hot tears melting my eyes. I watched her tiny fingers wiggle in slumber; I wanted to grab those fingers and smother them with kisses.

Her mother, who looked to be the same age as me, contemplated yogurt flavors while I stared like a crazy woman, my body smoldering with emotion. She noticed me and smiled. The acknowledgment startled me and I jumped, feeling like I'd been caught doing something wrong. I attempted a smile and slowly walked away, trying to seem as normal as possible.

The woman frowned and moved toward her daughter, unsure of my motives.

I felt like a complete whack job.

"I have a baby girl, too," I wanted to explain. "She's about the same age as your daughter. But she's in the car. I mean, I didn't just leave my baby in the car unattended. She's dead. Sitting in the front seat of my car."

Holy shit.

I was going crazy.

I pictured myself bringing Avery with me to the grocery store, placing the urn in the child seat and strapping her in. Or I could just put the urn in the infant carrier and place it on top of the cart the way most mothers did. I could even pull out the Baby Bjorn; she'd fit nicely in that.

Maybe I could get one of those big, pink, elastic baby hair

bows to dress her up. That would be good. That way everyone would know she was a girl. I laughed out loud at the thought of it, catching the curious eye of an old woman. I smiled sweetly and continued on my way.

I completed my shopping in a fog, tossing random things into my cart. It was more psychological than physical, but my womb literally ached, and it was impossible for me to concentrate on anything but the tenderness inside.

"I need to have another baby," I silently reflected. "Once I have another baby things will be okay again."

I'd thought about it many times since having Avery, but my trip to the store provided the epiphany. Having another baby would make everything better. I needed to get pregnant again, and I needed to do it as soon as possible. If I had a baby, the aching would finally go away.

Once I had a baby to take home with me, to hug and kiss and cuddle and love and take to the grocery store, I would be happy again.

*****

I was a crack addict looking for my next fix.

"Chris, we need to have another baby. Like, now," I pleaded, my eyes heady with desire.

"We will."

"You don't understand. We need to do it now."

"We can't do it now. The doctor said to wait."

I knew he was right, that it was risky for me to get pregnant so soon. But I wanted to be reckless, to throw away the logic and just do what felt right.

"But I need it," I coaxed, rubbing his shoulders and breathing down his neck, hoping to seduce him away from common sense.

"It hasn't even been a month yet. We have to wait," he said, pulling away from my touch.

"Fine," I pouted, stomping out of the room like an angry teenager. "Be an asshole about it, see if I care."

Like a good junkie, I was determined to find a way to get what I wanted, and I wasn't ready to take no for an answer.

*****

"What if my uterus doesn't work anymore?" I posed, climbing into bed the following evening. It was a question that had plagued me since Avery's delivery, and I figured I could use it for leverage.

Chris rolled over and stared at me, a step ahead of my game. "I'm sure your uterus works just fine."

"But what if it doesn't? What if it takes a really long time to get pregnant again? Maybe we should start trying now." I did my best to look sad and serious.

"What if it doesn't take a really long time? What if you get pregnant right away and something bad happens again because we didn't wait?"

I couldn't handle anything bad happening again, and the thought terrified me. Yet I was still blinded by baby fever. "What if nothing bad happens, and we finally get a baby we can keep?"

Chris was silent. I stared at him long and hard, unwilling to back down.

I needed a baby to feel whole again. I wanted to say it, to admit the truth behind my motives to the man I loved, but I couldn't. I was too afraid of disclosing my vulnerability.

Chris finally spoke, always a man of reason. "It's almost August. Daryl and Nicky are getting married at the beginning of November. We should wait until the wedding. Then we can start trying."

We were both standing up in the wedding, and I knew waiting was the smart thing to do. But I was tired of being smart. Where had it gotten me with Avery?

Maybe I could get him drunk enough to knock me up.

But then again, maybe he was right.

"Fine," I acquiesced, turning out the light.

Evidently, if I wanted immediate gratification, I was going to have to get it from a man other than my husband. As impulsive as I was, I wasn't quite ready to turn to adultery.

I started counting the days until November.

CHAPTER SEVENTEEN

The following week I ventured out of the house again, but this time I managed to leave Avery at home. The start of a new school year was just weeks away, and, while my primary obsession was babies, both dead and alive, I was sane enough to realize I needed supplies for work. I woke extra early that day, determined to get to Target as soon as the store opened, hoping to avoid meeting anyone I knew.

I didn't get the memo saying that every new mom takes their baby shopping at the ass-crack of dawn.

As I negotiated the aisles with my little red cart, I was surrounded. Tiny babies, fat babies, happy babies, screaming babies—everywhere I looked, babies, babies, babies. I was sure I was being mocked, like the universe was taking the one thing I couldn't have and shoving it in my face. "Look what you almost had," it taunted. "Look what you don't have."

Baby boys were tough to see, but baby girls were unbearable. I found myself transfixed by them, like the creepy woman you see on the news who steals someone else's kid.

I'd never do that, I thought to myself.

Or would I?

I was scaring myself, questioning my own sanity.

Before long I noticed other mothers staring at me, bothered by my peculiar behavior. They seemed so smug, so superior to me. They had succeeded where I had failed. I wanted to tell them that I was a mother too, that I also had a daughter. I was a member of their elite club—my membership badge just looked a little different. But I kept my mouth shut and averted my eyes, partly to stop being creepy but also so they couldn't see my tears.

I started to feel woozy and warm, like I might pass out. I took a few deep breaths and steadied myself with the cart, trying to find something resembling calm.

Breathe in, breathe out. Breathe in, breathe out.

I was going to have to get used to this, I told myself. In three weeks I would be back at work. Life was going to move on whether I was ready or not. If I was going to stay in it, I couldn't let my emotions take over.

I felt terrible but pushed on, determined to be strong. I did my best to ignore everyone around me, feigning ignorance and keeping my eyes focused on the aisle in front of me. I stared at my purse as I passed the baby girls' clothing; seeing the tiny little flowered dresses and pink ruffles would destroy me.

Focused on my task, I made quick work of my list. Before checking out I made a last-minute decision to run through the women's clothing section. I was tired of my clothes not fitting and needed some temporary outfits for my larger size.

I rifled through a display rack of t-shirts looking for a large. After no luck on the highest two, I squatted down to search the lowest shelf, where I found what I was looking for.

I grabbed the black tee and instantly panicked: I'd forgotten about my legs. They were stronger, but that was a relative term. Once in the kneeling position it was still impossible for me to stand up again without help.

Here I was, in the middle of Target, stuck on my knees. An employee walked by; I flashed a nervous smile and pretended to look for another size. Should I ask her for help? What would I say?

"Excuse me, miss…my baby died and it really fucked my legs up. Can you help me stand?"

I couldn't do it.

I looked at my cart, parked a few feet away. I crawled to it, stretching my arms high to grasp the handle. Placing the majority of my weight on my arms, like a fat kid on the monkey bars, I pulled with what little strength I had, grunting like a Russian weightlifter. It was a strange angle, but it was working. I was almost erect when—*WHOOSH*—the cart did a wheelie and sent me tumbling backward. I landed hard on my ass, right back where I started. I wiped the sweat from my brow, looking around to see if anyone had witnessed my accident. I was safely concealed by rows of cheap clothing made in Taiwan.

I giggled as I processed the absurdity of the situation. I was sitting in the middle of a crowded store stuck on my behind like an invalid. I didn't know whether I should laugh or cry, but I desperately wanted to call Chris and have him come and save me. Unfortunately, that wasn't a realistic option.

I started examining my choices. If using the cart wasn't going to work, I would have to try the t-shirt display. I crawled to it and shook the shelving unit, testing its sturdiness. It wobbled clumsily, but it was the only option. I inhaled and pushed, burdening the middle shelf with the entire weight of my chubby post-baby body. Both my arms and the shelving shook fiercely, but I pressed on, determined to stand. With one last grunt I was erect, just in time to watch the shelving unit crash to the floor with a loud bang, turning the rainbow of tees into a giant heap of cotton.

I stood motionless, a deer caught in the headlights. I turned to my left, then to my right. I saw no one. Red and panting, my face glistening with sweat, I tiptoed to my shopping cart and headed to checkout. Thankfully there was no line. I smiled nervously at the clerk, paid, and was on my way.

By the time I reached the parking lot tremors shook my body; by the time I opened the car door I was completely blind with hot tears. With great effort I crawled inside and flung myself to the seat, sobbing, defeated, longing to go back in time and fix my life, yearning to feel normal again. It was the loneliest I had ever been, and for the first time in my life, I wanted to die.

It was the only sure way my pain would come to an end—the only sure way I'd see my daughter again.

*****

For the next forty-eight hours I couldn't stop thinking of my own death. Until I lost Avery death was something I feared, something unknown I wanted to avoid at all costs. Before Avery I wasn't sure I believed in an afterlife, but now I had to believe I'd get a chance to see her again. I still found death scary, but I also looked forward to it, to a certain extent, since I figured my daughter would be waiting for me in that vast eternity where all good souls eventually end up.

I couldn't decide if I was truly suicidal, so I made a list of the various ways I could go to see if any tickled my fancy.

Slitting my wrists. Too messy. Did I even have the guts for that? And I couldn't make Chris clean that up.

Carbon monoxide. Would that ruin my car? I didn't want to ruin my car.

Hanging. I never passed that knot-tying course at summer camp.

Pills. I didn't have any. Where did people find that stuff?

Gun. I didn't have one of those either.

Poison. It seemed like an unreliable way to go.

I imagined driving off a highway overpass or down a boat ramp into a lake. I thought of jumping off a bridge or in front of an eighteen-wheeler.

There were so many ways to do it, but none of them seemed right for me.

The more I realistically considered dying, the sillier my idea became, and the less I wanted to do it. I was depressed and struggling, but I was sane enough to know that death wasn't the answer. My maternal grandmother took her own life shortly before I was born, and, though I never knew her, I witnessed the hole she left behind. I couldn't do that to my husband or my family.

I thought briefly about going to see a shrink or joining a support group. The hospital had a group for parents of miscarriage, stillbirth, and SIDS that met once a month, but

I couldn't imagine sitting in a circle with a bunch of other depressed people, sharing tales of our dead babies over coffee and donuts, trying to decide whose story was the most miserable. I had always been shy, an introvert at heart, and I just couldn't speak about Avery's death in a public forum.

I turned to my computer, where I found a surprisingly large network of support that allowed me to remain relatively unknown. I settled on joining two groups, one a global Facebook forum devoted to stillbirth, the other a BabyCenter group created just for parents who'd lost a child to an umbilical cord accident. They were anonymous enough that I felt comfortable sharing my feelings, yet supportive enough that I didn't feel as alone. But even with my newfound cyberfriends I was still searching for something more. I felt like Alice in Wonderland, hungering for a way back up the rabbit hole.

I finally forced myself to read the book my doctor gave me, hoping it would be therapeutic. It turned out to be a religious guide to loss, answering questions with scripture and offering ambiguous remarks about "God's plan" for those who died through miscarriage or stillbirth. Thankfully the book was short, because it pissed me off. While it was nice to think that my daughter was too good for our world, that she was so righteous and pure she was handpicked by God to fight in the eternal battle against evil, I didn't find any comfort in those concepts. The idea that my Avery was taken from me to save us all from the apocalypse wasn't a realistic explanation for why she died. I was looking for real, legitimate answers, not biblical scenarios.

The book also suggested that human beings don't have a soul until they are born, that the soul of a person arrives after they are released from the womb and enter life as we know it. If that were true, that meant my Avery was soulless. I couldn't accept that idea. My daughter was a real human being with a soul. She was just like every other baby born into this world, except she didn't have a beating heart.

I finished the book and tossed it aside, feeling worse.

I still blamed God for taking Avery away, but I started thinking about practical reasons why someone would want an innocent baby to die. That someone being God, of course. Maybe God was being merciful, and actually sparing her from a more terrible death later on.

Perhaps she was destined to be kidnapped and raped and buried in the woods, and she was being spared that horror. We were all spared that horror.

Maybe there was something physically wrong with her, like cancer, and God freed her from all of that extra suffering. By taking her at birth, we were saved having to watch her die later on.

We didn't know how long the cord had been wrapped around Avery's neck. If we had caught it in time to save her life, there was a chance she could have been severely retarded, maybe even braindead, which would have required a tortuous quality-of-life debate.

Maybe Avery actually saved us by making the decision for us. She made the decision to die so we didn't have to.

I decided there had to be other books that might provide me with better perspective on my situation, books that wouldn't leave me so angry and unfulfilled. I went on Amazon.com and typed the word "stillbirth" into the search window, and, surprisingly, my search returned over a hundred results. I was like a kid in a candy store as I studied the summaries, certain I would finally find closure through the words of someone else who had lost a child, my soul sister.

I chose three books and paid $20 extra for overnight shipping.

The answers I longed for were finally coming—not from God or a doctor or a support group, but from UPS.

When the box arrived, it was like Christmas morning; I tore through the packaging, eagerly contemplating which book to read first. I picked the thinnest of the three and curled up on the couch, certain happiness and understanding lay somewhere between those crisp white pages. After the first twenty pages, I threw the book on the floor in disgust. It read like a manual, starting out with medical descriptions of miscarriage, stillbirth, and infant death. Then it listed the steps that should be taken while in the hospital after each occurrence.

I didn't need a dictionary definition of what had happened to me, and I sure as hell was way past the hospital.

I picked up another book. As I flipped through the pages, more disappointment set in. The book was supposed to be about stillbirth, but it focused on miscarriage and lumped the two together. In both instances a woman loses a child, and miscarriage is no doubt traumatic, but to me they are worlds apart. I carried my baby in my belly for thirty-eight weeks. I felt her move. I went into labor, and I held her full-term body in my arms. It was not a miscarriage, and I was insulted that the author of this so-called book about coping with stillbirth treated it like it was.

The third book was what I had been hoping for: an actual story of a woman's personal experience with stillbirth. I spent the afternoon reading, comparing her pain to my own, her thoughts to my thoughts. The book made me feel a better in that it made me feel less alone, reading the words of someone else who had lost her daughter full-term. There were many similarities to our stories, and, while I relished the fact that someone else had been through what I'd experienced, I was still disappointed. The author's words were very controlled, very sterile, lacking the raw emotion I was feeling, the helplessness and isolation. I wanted to hear that she walked around the house with her dead child in her arms. I wanted her to admit that in the dark moments of despair she screamed at the top of her lungs and threw things at the walls. I wanted to hear that she was as crazy as I was. Yet she was calm with her loss, so utterly sane.

At the end of the book, what was left of my heart dropped. Shortly after she lost her daughter, the author became pregnant again.

She had another stillbirth.

I grabbed my computer and did a quick search, landing on the website of the Stillbirth Alliance. I scanned through the articles until I found one titled "Prediction and Prevention of Recurrent Stillbirth."

I felt an onslaught of panic as I read the words I was afraid of: A woman who has had a stillbirth is two to ten times more likely to have another if she gets pregnant again.

I sat on the couch, unable to breathe, fear pumping through my veins. What if this happened again? I couldn't go through another pregnancy only to give birth to another dead baby. I was already hanging by a thread; if I had another loss, I would shatter.

The thought burned the corners of my skull. My head pounded.

What if I never had a living child?

I closed the book and ascended the stairs to Avery's room, where I continued the strange ritual of taking my daughter from her shelf, giving her urn a hug and a kiss. I carried her to the rocking chair and sat down, lost in deep thought. What if this was all I would ever have, a child I couldn't see or touch or love directly?

Nina padded into my room and climbed onto my lap, rubbing her whiskered cheek against Avery in a feline hello. The three of us rocked silently for hours. My sadness shifted, and I once again found myself stewing with anger. Anger at God, at myself, and at all of the perfect people in the world with their perfect living babies.

My life would never be perfect without Avery.

As the sun fell behind the ancient oak in our backyard, I heard the garage door open. I gently pushed Nina off of my lap and sighed. I gave Avery one last kiss, closed the door, and headed downstairs to be a wife.

*****

At my six-week checkup, I was certain the doctor would tell me something was horribly wrong with me and I would never be able to have another child. The week leading up to my appointment, I tossed and turned each night, plagued by the idea that my uterus was somehow broken, or that the blood coursing through my veins was poison to my offspring.

But everything was fine.

My pap smear was fine. The substantial amount of blood work done came back normal, and Avery's autopsy results showed nothing out of the ordinary. Medically she was a healthy, normal baby girl, except for the umbilical cord bound tightly around her neck.

I was shaking as the doctor handed me a small white envelope containing the autopsy results.

"These are for you," she said softly. "Take them home, put them somewhere until you're ready to look at them. And if you never want to look at them, that's fine, too."

The paper felt heavy in my hands as I stared at the envelope containing The Truth, the answers I had been so frantically seeking for more than a month. Or at least some of the answers. It didn't cover the why, but it did cover the how, and that was one step closer.

As Chris and the doctor talked about the preventative measures we would take in my next pregnancy, their voices were a million miles away. I stared at the sealed envelope, longing to rip it open and devour the information.

"Right, Heid?" Chris asked.

I looked up to find my husband looking at me. "Oh, yeah, right." I smiled nervously, unsure what I was agreeing to.

We left the office through the waiting room this time, and I couldn't help but stare at the pregnant women seated uncomfortably in their chairs. Even in their discomfort they radiated a certain happiness, the beautiful bliss that only comes from carrying a child.

"That's going to be me soon," I thought as we walked to our car. "Soon we'll have another baby, and everything will be okay again..."

I had the envelope open before Chris started the car.

He laughed as I unfolded the documents. "Somehow I didn't think we were going to wait to open it."

I scanned the autopsy results, an analysis of my daughter's organs and a jumble of medical terms I sporadically understood. But I kept seeing the word "normal," and that was what mattered.

"At least she was healthy." I smiled sadly. "At least she was normal and healthy. It was just an accident."

A terrible, life-altering accident.

I read the pathologist's conclusion:

"The pertinent autopsy findings are found primarily with the placenta. There is a thrombosis of all three cord blood vessels that caused asphyxia and death in utero. The thrombosis was due to the tight nuchal cord. There are reactive changes seen within the placenta, lung, and thymus that are clearly due to asphyxia, and these include the marked erythroblastosis seen within both placental and lung vasculature spaces and the depletion of cortical lymphocytes within the thymus. These changes are typical of a fetal response to asphyxia."

The original speculation was correct. My daughter's cinched umbilical cord had cut off her oxygen supply from the placenta, eventually causing her death.

I breathed a sigh of relief as I thumbed through the pages. Nothing was wrong with me, nothing was wrong with her. I should be able to have another healthy child.

I froze as I read the final page in the packet, the delivering doctor's dictation. It was his account of that fateful night, from the second he saw me in the triage area to Avery's delivery. It had only been six weeks, but it seemed like an eternity had passed, and it was excruciating to relive those three days through his words.

But Avery was normal.

I was normal.

I folded the documents and neatly placed them back into the envelope. For a moment it seemed like everything was going to be okay, that my world was slowly righting itself.

I grabbed Chris's hand and squeezed. He turned and smiled, a genuine smile I hadn't seen in a while.

"Let's go out on the boat," I suggested, knowing he had been dying to hear those words. I was required to stay out of the water for six weeks after delivery and was bogged down with baby flab, so putting on a bathing suit hadn't been at the top of my list. But it was a beautiful day, and I had just received the all-clear to swim. Chris had the rest of the day off, so I figured it was time to become reacquainted with the Big Banana.

We packed our cooler with beer and sandwiches and headed out to the water, determined to have fun.

CHAPTER EIGHTEEN

HAPPY ONE-MONTH ANNIVERSARY TO YOUR BABY!

I stared at the card, perched atop the pile of mail I had just pulled from the box. It was from a formula company, and it came with a bunch of coupons and a list of milestones I could look forward to in the coming weeks.

It was refreshing to know my baby's first smile was just around the corner. I wondered if I'd be able to see it through the steel urn.

When I pre-registered at the hospital, I'd checked the box to receive coupons and other freebies for my baby. Evidently they didn't keep track of which babies died, since over the past few weeks I'd been with bombarded diaper coupons, formula samples, and parenting magazines.

But this was Avery's first birthday card. And it reminded me that she would never have birthdays.

I walked back to the house, my heart heavy with the unexpected memory of what I had lost.

I looked at the coupons; they didn't expire until 2010.

I threw them in a box filled with the other free baby crap I hoped to someday use.

*****

Time, which dripped slower than frozen molasses the first few weeks after Avery's death, began moving at a frantic pace, and before I knew it we were deep into August. I was left with two short weeks to pull myself together before I had to return to work and rejoin the real world. While I had good days and bad days, I always had sad days. I still couldn't go a full twenty-four hours without tears.

I often found myself staring in the mirror at the stranger reflected in the glass. To most people I looked the same, but I didn't recognize myself. My hair, once lustrous from an infusion of pregnancy hormones, was starting to thin out. My blue eyes were dull and lifeless, lost in a faraway place. My smile was forced, fake, my crow's feet more pronounced. My summer tan faded rapidly. I looked pale, tired, and old.

I knew I needed to do some major soul searching if I was going to survive my return to work, and I decided the best place for reflection was at the lake, the one place I felt free. For centuries water has had a spiritual connection. It cleanses the soul, washes away sins, and revives the spirit. I had never needed its healing power so badly, and I hoped the lake wouldn't let me down.

We spent my last two weeks of freedom on the boat, lazily drifting through the azure water, sipping cocktails and burying our troubles in the sand. On weekdays Chris would rush home from work at 5:01; I would be waiting with a quick dinner and a beach bag. We'd speed the two short miles to the lake, inhaling the last few hours of warm August sunshine until the final sliver of red vanished behind the towering pines on the western shore.

On weekends we were on the water by eleven in the morning, and we'd tieup at the sandbar, meet with friends, and do the things people with little kids can't do. Some days the alcohol flowed freely and I drank too much, but I was tired of feeling guilty about my life and tired of apologizing. I had been a saint my entire pregnancy, and I longed to once again feel like a normal human being.

Other days were more reclusive, and we'd park our boat in the middle of the lake, away from the revelry, letting the current direct our path. I'd lie on the back of the Big Banana and let the sun caress my skin, feeling the waves lap sluggishly against the sides of the boat, rocking me to sleep.

For the first six weeks after Avery's death, I didn't live. I went through the motions of life physically, but my mind, my soul, my heart—they were lost in the past. Being surrounded by water somehow brought me back from the dead and showed me life could still be beautiful.

I still mourned my baby girl, but the lake soothed my tired soul. I thought of Avery often, but not the desperate, helpless thoughts I was used to. For the first time since her death I stopped trying to find answers and just allowed myself to be.

And in being I began to see my daughter again.

I'd stare up at the brilliant sky and see Avery in a passing cloud, the condensed water vapor shifting into angels' wings for a split second, like I was the only person in the world meant to see it. A soft breeze would blow, and I would close my eyes and savor the sweet feel of it brushing my cheek, certain it was my daughter sending me a kiss from above. A dragonfly would land on my leg, and I knew Avery had stopped by to say hello.

I'd jump in the lake and feel her next to me, gliding parallel through the silky water. I glimpsed her red lips in every sunset, heard her sweet voice in every chirping bird, felt her innocence in every starlit night.

I thought of how Avery would never have to grow old or feel pain. Like the water swirling around my toes, she would remain eternally young, and that comforted me.

I felt Avery's presence more on the lake than anywhere else, and I began to realize that if I opened my eyes and looked around, she was still with me.

She would always be with me.

*****

My first day back at work was unbearable. I dreaded going back, which was ironic, since I loved my job. But I was nervous about the people, the questions, the stares. I taught high school; these kids had memories. What was I supposed to say to my students? Everyone knew I'd been pregnant, but did they know what actually happened? Or did they hear some twisted version of the story? Were people going to treat me differently? Would they whisper behind my back and think I was some sort of freak? I couldn't decide if I should directly address what happened or ignore it.

Thankfully there were no students at school the first week, only teachers and administrators. As I walked up the steps to the front door—still gingerly, though my legs were much better than before—I buried the impulse to turn around and go home.

It will get better, I told myself.

I was reminded of something my mother always said, words she used to console me over silly breakups with high school boyfriends and to calm my nerves before piano recitals. She whispered them again as I was lying in the hospital bed, grieving the loss of my firstborn.

"This too shall pass."

I was beginning to think she was full of shit.

I was greeted with sympathetic smiles and a slew of "I'm so sorry"s. One of my favorite coworkers wrapped me in a hug and said nothing else. Everyone was nice and very compassionate, but I was still paranoid. I was convinced that behind their kind words they were all judging me, questioning how I let what happened happen. I wanted to hold a press conference to explain the gory details of Avery's demise, to clarify my current mental state, to answer the questions I knew people had but weren't brave enough to ask to my face. Instead I smiled my best smile, graciously accepted their words with a thank you, and went about my business.

Our first meeting as a whole staff started happily, with the principal soliciting stories from the teachers about all the fun things they did over the summer. People raised their hands and shared stories of vacations to far-off places, volunteer work, and new hobbies. After fifteen minutes of titillating tales of summer fun, the room was once again silent.

"Anyone else?" the principal asked. "Anyone else do anything exciting?"

I was tempted to raise my hand. "I gave birth to a dead baby." But I refrained.

Eventually we were divided into small groups to do busy work that was supposed to make us better teachers. As we sat around the table chatting, the topic turned to children, somehow landing on how kids destroy a woman's body. A female teacher I didn't know very well pointed at me. "You just had a baby. What did that little girl do to you?" She laughed as she spoke, snorting a bit.

Evidently she thought she was a comedian.

The table fell silent; everyone shifted uncomfortably in their seats, eyes darting around the room, looking for an escape. I stared at my peers, their faces dumb with disbelief.

I wrestled with my words. Seconds seemed like hours and my cheeks burned. I decided to give her the benefit of the doubt and assume she hadn't gotten the memo. Swallowing the lump in my throat, I smiled sweetly, even throwing in a small laugh. "Oh yeah, she definitely did a number on me."

The tension at the table relaxed, and everyone immediately focused on our work again.

Our conversation didn't stray off topic for the rest of the day.

*****

By the end of the week I was feeling more comfortable in my own skin. I spent the first two days feeling naked and awkward, like everyone was looking at me and talking about me, but by the third I realized most people had moved on. People didn't care about my pain as much as I did; they had their own lives to obsess over. My fellow teachers were, for the most part, treating me like an ordinary person, and for the first time since the beginning of July I was finally beginning to feel normal. Work was a magnificent distraction that forced me to think about something other than my loss, to give my brain a vacation from unanswerable questions that wouldn't go away. Avery was always in the back of my mind, but her loss no longer governed my existence.

The night before the students returned to school I couldn't sleep, which happened every year. But this year it wasn't because I was going over lesson plans in my head. It was because I was rehearsing my "speech" over and over again. In two of my classes, the majority of students were kids I had the previous year, so they had watched Avery grow with me. As easy as it would be to ignore her death, I decided that as the adult it was my job to address the elephant in the room. These kids were teenagers, and they weren't stupid. I needed to talk about what happened if we were going to have any sense of normalcy in my classroom.

"I hope you guys all had a great summer." I smiled as my first class of students took their seats. I took a deep breath and sat down on the edge of my desk as the eager faces of my students, mostly girls, gazed up at me expectantly. "I think most have you have heard what happened with my daughter Avery—that I was pregnant and she died because of complications."

My classroom had never been so quiet. The only sounds were the humming of the computers, the faint buzzing of fluorescent lights, and the beating of my own nervous heart. A few students fidgeted uncomfortably; some had tears in their eyes. My stomach swirled with uncertainty as I struggled to continue.

"It was an accident, a terrible accident. The cord was wrapped around her neck, and they couldn't do anything about it," I continued quickly, trying to get it over with. "It was really hard for me, for us. It was really sad. I cried a lot, and I miss my daughter. But I want you to know that I'm okay, and I'm happy to be back here."

As I quickly wiped a tear from my eye, hoping no one noticed, one of my students leapt from her chair, running to the front of the room and wrapping me in her arms.

"I just need to give you a hug," she laughed, her voice cracking.

Teenagers can be cruel, self-centered, and indulgent, but they also have an amazing capacity to feel and give affection. I felt an excess of love in that room, and it reaffirmed my decision to share a piece of the darkest day of my thirty-one years.

Teenagers also have short attention spans, for which, for once, I was grateful. Within minutes my twenty-four students were smiling and laughing and talking about their summers, the dreadful tragedy of their teacher forgotten.

That first week still brought a number of awkward moments. In my Intro to Journalism class, a class made up primarily of freshman who knew absolutely nothing about me, we had a "get to know each other" activity. When a young man asked if I had any kids, I had to stop and think.

"No," I replied softly. "I don't have any kids." I felt an avalanche of guilt the second the words came out of my mouth, but how was I going to explain my situation to a pimply fourteen-year-old?

Walking down the hallway between classes, I spotted the smiling face of a former student, a sweet, shy girl who buried herself in fiction.

"Mrs. Chandler!" she exclaimed, running to catch up with me. "How's your baby?"

I hesitated, searching for the right words. I didn't want to traumatize the poor girl, but I didn't want to lie.

"Um, well, she didn't make it," I started, hoping that would be enough. She stared at me blankly. "There were problems, and she died."

Her face twisted into disbelief.

"Oh my God, Mrs. Chandler, I'm so sorry," she gasped, touching my shoulder. "Well, you have a good day."

I watched her nervously rush down the hall, wishing there was a manual on how to approach these situations. I couldn't lie about Avery, but the truth was so sad.

Dealing with students was complicated, but breaks in the staff lunchroom proved to be the most challenging part of my days. Listening to colleagues talk about their kids, especially the people who had new babies at home, tore my spirit. I listened quietly as they complained about poopy diapers and sleepless nights, feigning indifference, but I was dying inside and growing increasingly bitter.

Had they forgotten what happened to me? How could they be so damn insensitive? I didn't want people to walk on eggshells around me, but it hurt to listen to these women talk about the things I was supposed to be talking about, the things I would have been talking about if Avery had simply rolled a different direction.

I'd sit at the table and stare silently at my sandwich, adding to the conversation in my head.

"Wow, that sucks that your daughter is up all night," I imagined myself saying. "My daughter is such a great sleeper. She hasn't made a peep since she was born!"

I spent a lot of time talking to people in my head. When a student was distraught over her loser boyfriend, I consoled her, but in my head I said, "Really, kid? You think this is the end of the world? Do you have any idea how much worse your life could be?" When a mother was irate that her son's yearbook didn't have his name embossed on the cover, I was sweet and accommodating, but inside I said, "Yeah? Well my daughter died this summer. Talk to me about something that really fucking matters, lady." When a disappointed parent inquired how to get his son's grade up from an A-, I provided a logical, helpful answer, but in my head I said, "Are you fucking kidding me right now? Give your son a hug and a kiss, tell him you're proud, and be happy that he's alive."

Each day when people asked how I was doing I smiled and said *good*, but in my head I said, "I didn't wake up crying or feeling like slitting my wrists today, so that's a start!"

After that first week, however, it was like Avery never happened. I think people were thankful I didn't talk about her, and the sadness that first surrounded my return to school drifted away.

But I was torn.

I wanted to talk about Avery; I *needed* to talk about her. So often I longed to mention her in conversation, but I bit my tongue, not wanting to cause awkwardness and bring everyone else down. She was a huge part of my life, of who I had become, yet I swept her under the rug for everyone else's sake.

One day at the lunch table, which was typically all women, my fellow teachers were talking about C-sections. One turned to me and asked, "Did you have a C-section with Avery?" The conversation came to a halt and everyone stared uneasily, waiting for my reaction. At first I was stunned—not because I thought it was too personal, but simply because someone outside my family had acknowledged Avery's existence and even called her by name.

I smiled. "No, I didn't have a C-section," I answered, awkwardly delighted. "I did it the old-fashioned way."

I decided I wasn't giving people enough credit. They hadn't forgotten I lost my daughter; they just didn't talk about Avery because I never talked about Avery. I didn't speak of her because I didn't want to make people uncomfortable, but they weren't comfortable saying anything because I didn't. It was a vicious circle, one I had unintentionally kept rolling through my own fear. One that I was now determined to end.

CHAPTER NINETEEN

In the nine weeks before the 2008–2009 school year started, the days were dark and never-ending, each one an exhausting eternity filled with tears and regret. Back at work, with people talk to, friends to laugh with, and more to think about than sadness, the days quickly melted into weeks. Each day was a little brighter, and each day I grew a little stronger.

Until my iPod tried to kill me.

I was driving home from work on a sunny, early autumn day, windows down, speakers blaring like a teenager. I happily belted out the All-American Reject's "Move Along," followed by Kid Rock's latest overplayed hit, "All Summer Long."

The music player was on shuffle, randomly selecting songs for me on its own technological whim, and it decided to slow things down. I literally stopped breathing when the next song started—"Fix You" by Coldplay.

I had fallen in love with the song in 2005 on an overly dramatic episode of *The O.C.*, and it was the first time I had heard it since Avery's death.

I bit my lip as Chris Martin's haunting voice chanted through the speakers, singing of lights guiding and bones igniting. I couldn't help picturing Avery's tiny body being shoved into a furnace, bursting into flames, her bones slowly crumbling to dust. I struggled to drive on, sobbing hysterically.

If only I could've fixed Avery, my life would be so different. But how do you fix something you didn't know was broken?

I carelessly wiped snot on my sleeve as Martin sang of streaming tears and losing irreplaceable things, barely keeping my monstrous mom-mobile in its own lane. *Could it be worse?* the song asked me. Could it?

"No," I gasped. "It couldn't be worse."

I drove another mile, completely blinded by tears, running a red light and nearly crushing a pedestrian. I finally pulled off into a liquor store parking lot and slammed the car into park, inches away from a light post.

Yet I couldn't bring myself to change the song. I sat in the parking lot and bawled, oblivious to the curious glances of passersby, eventually playing the song again.

And again.

And again.

By the fifth time my tears were mostly dry, and I felt competent enough to operate a motor vehicle.

Once home I attached the music player to my computer and rifled through hundreds of songs, deleting the ones I thought might inspire breakdowns.

"Fix You"—deleted.

Colbie Caillat's "Capri"—gone.

Sarah McLachlan's "Angel"—erased.

Puff Daddy's "I'll Be Missing You"—toast.

I thought I had myself covered, but a week later I called in sick after a full thirty minutes of weeping in the garage, "Your Guardian Angel" by The Red Jumpsuit Apparatus blasting from my car stereo. Thinking about my own guardian angel was just too much for me that morning.

Ah, the power of music.

*****

I awoke to darkness, thoughts surging in my head like floodwaters through a broken levee. I opened my nightstand drawer and rifled blindly through the mess, feeling my way to a small notebook and pen.

My chest pounded as I ran to the bathroom and shut the door, crouched on the floor, and wrote for hours, feverishly, manically. My vision blurred and my fingers burned, but I pressed on. I felt stopping would be the death of me.

When I finally crawled back into bed, panting and exhausted, the birds were waking.

I had no idea what had just happened, but I slept better than I had in months.

This bizarre routine continued for weeks—not nightly, but enough that I began to question my own sanity and long for a full night's rest.

And then, just as suddenly as it came on, the writing stopped. I kept waiting for it to return, for the three a.m. fever to come and send me scurrying hysterically to the corner, but it was gone. My mind was empty, my notebook full, my soul purged. A peculiar sense of relief washed over me, like I had somehow buried every last piece of guilt and regret within those pages.

Had I?

I picked up the notebook and flipped through the sheets. It was barely legible, the crazed chicken scratch of a mad woman possessed by her own ghost, but the words were mine.

Lost, floating sideways. Will it end? When? How? Who?

Gone. All gone. Never to return. No flesh, no bones, no eyes, no cries, no smiles, hugs, kisses, love, just GONE. GONE. GONE.

We aren't supposed to bury our children.

How? Why? What did I do? What did she do? What did we do? Could it have been changed, helped, stopped, different? Destiny, fate, or bad luck? Is there an alternate universe where we are alive and happy?

Most of the pages were so sad, so lost, yet it was me in those pages. Those were my feelings, my life reflected in that black ink. I skipped to the last page.

We aren't supposed to live in the past. WE WILL DROWN.

I read those words again and again, so often that I began to trust them. I wasn't ready to drown, so I decided it was time I learned to live in the present.

*****

Before long it was officially fall, my favorite season, and life was a whirlwind of football games, cider mills, and chilly nights by the campfire. My legs gradually grew stronger. I started running again, something I thought I'd never be able to do, and it was liberating. I was no longer afraid to climb stairs or squat down in superstores. I instantly lost twenty pounds, half of my lingering baby weight. I went from crying daily to crying weekly to not really crying much at all.

Chris and I spent all of our free time together, an inseparable unit that had somehow managed to weather the ugliest storm. For a brief moment I had worried that losing Avery would tear us apart, but she brought us closer. We went out often, always together, frequenting our favorite restaurants and bars and attending and hosting parties.

I found myself feeling like the old me, the woman who smiled and laughed and danced until dawn. But I had to watch myself, to be extra careful, for occasionally I'd have one drink too many and be blindsided by grief, collapsing into a blubbering mess on the floor of a public bathroom stall, weeping for my daughter.

We surrounded ourselves with good friends, people with whom we could talk freely of Avery. From day one I was amazed at how easily Chris spoke of her, how he wove her name into conversation so effortlessly that it was never weird. I was always self-conscious when I said her name, but before long I began to open up. Speaking of my daughter, at least to a select group of friends, became routine. She was a part of our lives, so it was inevitable that she became part of our friends' lives, too. I realized I had to talk; talking kept me sane and kept Avery real.

While life in our inner circle was easy, I still had a hard time addressing people who didn't know. At a party with my husband's work friends, I shocked a coworker's wife when she asked how things were going with my new baby.

"Yeah," I started, taking a gulp of my Sangria. "Things didn't really go that well…"

As I gave my synopsis she radiated discomfort, her eyes wide. She swiftly finished her drink and excused herself.

I sighed as she walked away. I was growing used to it, but it was tough being a pariah, the person with the scarlet letter that people couldn't wait to get away from. I thought I needed to start wearing a big red "S" on my chest to warn people of my stillbirth.

Parent-teacher conferences also provided plenty of awkward moments. A few parents had heard, but most were clueless. As part of our chitchat parents typically asked if I had any children of my own. I wanted to be true to myself and to Avery, so I was honest. But when I said I had a daughter who died just before her due date, it made some people so distressed that I decided to simply start saying no.

It was a lie, and I cringed every time I said it, but it made my job easier.

I often found simple everyday tasks like going to the dentist or the grocery store tricky. No one expected simple small talk to result in a miserable story about the death of a baby girl, but that's what people got with me. The truth took people by surprise and the conversation would screech to a painful halt, but I couldn't blame them. It was a horrible story—a story I had lived—and it *should* make people sad. But I always ended up feeling at fault for the awkward situation, like by not sugarcoating the truth I had done something wrong. I always apologized and desperately tried to save the conversation. "I'm okay with it, though, really," I would lie. "Everything happens for a reason."

I felt awful around pregnant friends and coworkers and did my best to avoid them; in my mind, I was a walking bad omen, a constant reminder that something could go wrong with their baby. I shouldn't be the one feeling bad, I told myself. I was the one with the dead baby. Theirs was probably going to live a long, happy life. Yet I couldn't get past the feeling that I was the grim reaper for the unborn.

Despite all of the awkward moments, in between the guilt, the head chatter, and the tricky conversations, I was no longer ruled by grief and crippled by desperation. It happened over a matter of months, so gradually that it came as a surprise. I started laughing more, smiling more, living more. Anger faded; hope grew.

I could go to the store without being paralyzed by the sight of babies. I could actually look at babies and not cry. I rarely had the urge to scream "My daughter's dead" in crowded places. I found myself thinking of a future rather than dwelling on a past I could not change. My heart, which had walked out of that hospital room with my dead daughter, began to grow again, making room for more love in my life.

Time didn't make the pain go away, but it made remembering a little easier. The pain remained, but it became different. The grief didn't stop, but it changed. I missed my daughter and thought about her hourly, but I was learning that I could love her, miss her, and still experience happiness. Moving on didn't mean I was forgetting Avery. Avery was always there; she always will be. But I couldn't let her death be the death of my soul.

She wouldn't want that.

CHAPTER TWENTY

In November 2008, just over four months after Avery's birth, I was pregnant again. Unlike the first time, this pregnancy was completely mapped out. My best friend was married November 6; I calculated I would be ovulating that day. I was a bridesmaid, Chris a groomsman. We ate, drank, and danced the night away, then retired to our hotel room and had crazy, drunken, planned sex.

Three weeks later I peed on a stick and got two pink stripes.

When I got pregnant with Avery, I was a nervous wreck, riddled with anxiety over becoming a mother. I worried I wouldn't be good at it, that I wouldn't have enough love for my daughter. I didn't know what to expect that first time, so the magic of my pregnancy was overshadowed by fear.

But that all changed when I saw my daughter. I instantly loved her more than anything, and I knew I would be an incredible mother if I could only have one more chance.

By my second pregnancy, I wanted a baby so badly, was supposed to have a baby, that being pregnant again gave me an eerie sense of calm, like all was once again right with the world. I had an easy glow about me, and I smiled more than I had in months.

My composure held through the first half of my pregnancy. Chris and I painstakingly decided to go to the same OBGYN as we had for Avery, but we asked to only see the female doctor instead of being rotated amongst the three. It was a difficult decision, but it was aided by the knowledge that she was a good doctor and was already emotionally involved with us. While I'd tossed around the blame card after Avery's death, I had to believe the doctors did all they could with the information they had. And I truly believed my doctor would go to the ends of the earth to put a healthy baby in my arms.

This time no one was surprised to find out I was pregnant; everyone expected it to happen sooner rather than later. From our parents to our friends to my students, they all told us they had been waiting for it, that they "just knew" we'd try again. Still, I was taken aback by how many people told me how strong I was for getting pregnant so soon after Avery. To me there wasn't any other option; it was either dive in headfirst or never do it again.

And I had to do it again.

As with Avery, I felt normal and had no morning sickness. I was a little tired, but other than that, my fast-growing waistline was the only indicator I was having another child. I gained thirty-five pounds on top of the twenty I still had to lose from Avery. I was fat, but I was fat and happy.

Chris was constantly on edge, expecting the worst to happen because the worst had happened. I, on the other hand, walked around in a fog of tranquility, punch-drunk on a cocktail of hormones and love for the blossoming bean in my belly. I knew everything was going to be okay. Everything had to be okay—there wasn't any other option. This baby had a guardian angel, the littlest angel in heaven watching from above.

Avery wouldn't let anything go wrong. I just knew it.

I spent a lot of time in Avery's room, talking to my daughter. I'd hold her urn up to my growing belly, hoping some magical force would come through and protect her new sibling. I thanked her for being such a good big sister and explained that she would be moving rooms when the new baby came. (We decided to keep her on the dresser in our room.)

I leafed through her closet, all of the tiny pink clothes I had left on their hangers. I shivered with excitement at the thought of finally having someone to put them on. I pulled out a blue-

and-pink gingham romper and a yellow-and-white flowered sundress, squealing with delight.

"You are going to look so cute in these!" I exclaimed, rubbing my belly. "I can't wait for you to get here."

I knew scientifically there was a fifty-fifty chance, but I was convinced I would be having a girl. It was the natural order of things. My life had been tipped off its axis by Avery's death. I'd been struggling to find my footing in an off-kilter world, hanging by a thread and drifting sideways through the universe, desperately trying not to barrel out of control. My world was almost back to normal, and it would surely right itself with the birth of my next baby.

My baby girl.

I would finally have redemption.

When Chris and I sat down in the waiting room for my twenty-week appointment, the gender appointment, I was uncharacteristically quiet. I sat on my hands, trying to hide the shaking. The longer I waited, the more nervous I became, and I could feel the hives of anxiety. My breathing was heavy, labored by the lump of panic in my throat. I'd never experienced an anxiety attack before, but I was well on my way.

Chris, always overly concerned during this pregnancy, was disturbed by my peculiar behavior. "What's wrong?" he whispered, taking my hand. "Are you gonna be okay?"

I hesitated, carefully searching for the right words. "I'm excited. And scared. And I just want to get this over with."

I couldn't bear to tell him I was terrified that I might not be having a girl.

He smiled, lovingly putting his arm around my hunched shoulders. "Everything is going to be fine. It doesn't matter if it's a boy or a girl, all that matters is that it's healthy, right?"

I slowly nodded my head in agreement, wishing I could honestly say that was true.

My ultrasound was before my doctor's appointment, and as we walked into the dark room I was in a dream, stumbling through a dark forest. I silently lay on the table as Chris took his seat next to me, intent on the image of our unborn child and asking the technician questions as she worked. I was lost in my own thoughts, their voices a distant sound too far away to distinguish.

Only when there was silence did I realize someone was talking to me.

"Are you ready?" the tech repeated, giving me a smile.

I looked at Chris, shifting in his chair, folding and unfolding his hands in anticipation. I could tell he could care less what we were having; he was just ecstatic that everything looked okay with our second child. I felt a surge of guilt. I should be open, too, but I couldn't feel that way. I desperately wanted a girl, someone to replace the baby that was stolen from me that July day.

I held my breath for a moment, struggling to find poise. I would not let my emotions get the best of me.

"All right, let's do it," I said, raising my eyebrows and faking a smile.

I stared at the screen as the Doppler cruised across my stomach. I flashed back to a year earlier, on that same table in the same dark room with the same ultrasound technician. "It's a girl," she had said with a smile. I still heard her words echoing in my head. I looked around, reminding myself that it was a different year and a different pregnancy.

This baby was not Avery.

"Okay, right there," she announced, pointing at the screen. "You're having a little boy!"

I closed my eyes as her words crashed over me, unable to breathe.

A boy.

I was having a boy.

I didn't want a boy.

I wanted a girl.

"Congratulations," the tech gushed. "Boys are so much fun."

Chris stood to help me off the table, a schoolboy smile pasted on his face. He was glowing, and I saw visions of Little League and peewee football dancing in his head.

I smiled weakly, but my heart had again been ripped from my chest. This wasn't what was supposed to happen—it was all wrong. I was supposed to have a girl, a sweet baby girl that I could hold forever, not just for a day.

As we returned to the waiting room to wait for my appointment with the doctor, I could feel the misery drowning my body.

Don't cry, don't cry, don't cry...

I usually had excellent restraint with my emotions, but as my wide butt hit the vinyl chair, a hot tear trickled down the left side of my face. In my right eye, a puddle formed, and my bottom eyelid was not a sufficient dam to keep it at bay. Before long I was crying, not the happy tears of an expectant mother but bitter tears of disappointment. I stared silently at the wall, hoping no one would notice.

While I clearly wanted a girl, I hadn't expected to have such a strong reaction to having a boy. I'd wanted a boy, too, but not now. Now I needed to have a girl. I felt it in every cell of my body, an ache so urgent nothing else could satisfy it.

But was it really a new baby girl I wanted so badly, or was I just still looking for Avery? My body was ready for another baby after four months, but I still had a long way to go emotionally.

It wasn't long before Chris noticed my tears. "What's wrong?" he gasped, reaching for my hand. "Why are you crying?"

"I don't know, nothing," I sobbed quietly, trying to avoid being noticed by anyone else. The room was so damn quiet. I gave Chris a pathetic smile, trying to convince him that my weeping was just silly girl stuff.

He frowned. He knew me too well. He knew I didn't like to cry, and I never cried in public. "Something's wrong. Are you sad that we're having a boy?"

Hearing Chris speak those words sent more tears gushing. After all we'd been through, it was so cruel of me to be disappointed, to be heartbroken because I was having a boy. I was selfish to feel that way, and I felt phenomenally guilty.

But I couldn't help how I felt.

I stared at my husband, patiently awaiting an answer. I reluctantly nodded, biting my lower lip to keep any stray sobs locked in my throat. "I really wanted a girl," I confessed.

He wrapped his arms around me, nonchalantly drying off my sodden face. "We'll have another girl someday." He smiled, running his fingers through my hair. "Just not this time."

He handed me the ultrasound pictures, and I couldn't help but smile too. At twenty weeks, my little boy was a tiny, perfectly formed person, with chubby cheeks just like his big sister. Even though he was a boy, I couldn't help but love him.

I just couldn't stop myself from wondering if I would have loved him even more if he were a girl.

*****

When I told my mom I was having a boy, I could sense her disappointment. My brother already had two boys, so Avery would have been the first princess in the family. Now we were adding another little prince.

The more I thought about it, however, the more the idea of having a boy grew on me. While I looked like a girly girl, I was a tomboy at heart. My youth was spent in the great outdoors, fishing and playing with Tonka trucks; as an adult, I still loved sports. My friends all said I was going to be the perfect mom for a little boy, and I knew they were right. I envisioned crisp fall Saturday mornings tailgating with the little guy before football games and teaching him how to fill out his bracket for March Madness.

Maybe having a boy was just what I needed.

As I sorted through my feelings, I realized that having a boy also gave me a semblance of closure I wouldn't have gotten with a girl. It was difficult to have another child so close to Avery's death, and I had wanted another girl because I hoped she could replace Avery. But Avery couldn't be replaced, and this little boy was teaching me that. With him inside my belly, I was able to appreciate that he was his own person, as Avery had been her own person. She wasn't something that could be swapped out with the birth of another baby.

*****

It took another two months for me to be ready to work on the baby's room. Avery's old room.

The walls were a neutral celery color, so we didn't need to paint. I looked at the curtains and the bedding, so pink and frilly and girly, and knew that just about everything needed to be packed away. I purchased five giant plastic tubs and reluctantly went to work.

I packed the clothes first, doing my best to group everything by size without spending too much time thinking, since a memory was attached to virtually every piece of clothing. I salvaged a few unisex items, but the rest went in bins. I packed pink "princess" picture frames, two ceramic piggy banks embossed with Avery's name, and a giant pink ladybug pillow. I packed pink pacifiers, ruffled booties no bigger than my thumb, stacks of monogrammed pink blankets.

I worked silently, quickly, trying to pack everything safely away before I realized what I was doing. But I already understood. For the past eleven months, I'd held on to a fantasy. By keeping Avery's room decorated and her clothes waiting, I kept the dream alive, the dream that maybe someday I would finally bring her home. Through dismantling her room I was finally, truly, painfully accepting reality. Avery would never sleep on the ladybug sheets. She would never wear the pink polka-dot bathing suit with matching sunglasses. Maybe someday a little girl would, but that little girl would not be Avery. It was a final goodbye, and though it hurt like hell, it needed to be done.

Tears inevitably fell, but I refused to let them distract me from my strange farewell ceremony. I felt my little boy kick, a soft, sweet flutter tickling my insides, and I pushed on. Within an hour the room was stripped clean, save a few gender-neutral stuffed animals. A handful of white onesies hung in the closet waiting for the next child, the dresses, ruffles, and all things pink neatly tucked away for another day. One by one I moved the boxes into a spare bedroom closet.

I returned to the room and was comforted by its simplicity. I was sad yet relieved that the job I dreaded was finally complete. I had purged the heartache and pain left behind by my first child and was ready to love again, ready to give this new baby, my son, my entire heart.

I gently took Avery from the shelf and gave her a hug. "You're going to be a great big sister," I whispered softly.

We headed downstairs to my bedroom, her new resting place.

CHAPTER TWENTY-ONE

The remainder of my pregnancy was relatively uneventful. There were no mysterious bird deaths on my doorstep, no winged kamikazes on suicide missions in front of my SUV.

The end was also very quiet.

Avery had four baby showers; people were always oohing and ahhing and providing their insight on raising a little girl. No one offered to throw a shower for my son. He received no tiny outfits, no stuffed animals, no monogrammed gifts prior to his birth. People kept their advice to themselves. It was as if the world was holding its collective breath until they were certain my son would live.

My previous stillbirth made me "high risk," so I was monitored closely during the third trimester. I appreciated the extra care, but I couldn't help being angry that my first child had to die to receive the premium prenatal package the next time around. It might not have been true, but in my mind Avery would have lived if I'd had that extra care—hell, she might have lived if I could have had just one or two more ultrasounds.

I'm sure the insurance companies have done countless analysis of statistics and dollar signs that prove it would be a phenomenal waste of money to give every pregnant woman special treatment, and they're probably right. But as a lifetime member of the small percentage of the population that has had a stillbirth, I can honestly say you can't put a dollar sign on a child's life. I would pay millions if it meant my daughter could walk this earth, healthy and alive. Instead I get to haul my daughter around the house in a container we bought at Hobby Lobby.

Mondays were ultrasounds with biophysical profiles, where they checked for movement, breathing, and amniotic fluid levels. To keep us sane, they also located the umbilical cord, making sure it wasn't in the wrong place, although I often wondered what they would do if it was.

I was afraid to ask.

Thursdays were non-stress tests, where I was able to hear my son's heartbeat for an entire half an hour. He was a lazy boy who, like his sister, didn't move much, so the nurses stuffed me with donuts to get the little guy kicking.

It seemed like I was always at the doctor, because I was, but the extra supervision saved me. While I skated through the first thirty weeks of pregnancy on cloud nine, as the end neared I was a paranoid mess.

School was out, so I had a lot of extra time on my hands. I tried to stay busy, to keep my troubled mind from cataloging everything that could go wrong, but it was in vain. When you've been through hell and back, it's just not possible to have faith that everything will turn out fine. I'd leave the doctor on Thursday beaming with confidence in my baby's health; by Sunday night I was positive something had gone horribly wrong and his little heart had stopped beating. Monday's BPP eased my fears, but by Wednesday I was counting the hours until the non-stress test. Without these extra appointments, I would've demanded to be checked into the hospital for the last six weeks of my pregnancy.

At thirty-four weeks we discussed the "plan" with my doctor. Chris and I had decided that, psychologically, we just couldn't wait around for my body to go into labor naturally. Chris was even more paranoid, and the two of us were a walking doomsday of what-ifs. My doctor said she would induce me at exactly thirty-eight weeks, not one day sooner, so we made my appointment for July 21. Putting a date on the calendar made me feel better, like there was finally an end to the rollercoaster ride with Baby #2.

Carter, my son, was going to be here July 21.

I just had to keep him alive until then.

The night of June 30 I couldn't sleep. It was the one-year anniversary of my water breaking, 365 days removed from the night our lives changed forever. I rested my head against my damp pillow and watched the bright green numbers on the clock silently tick forward, listening to the measured breathing of my husband. I hated him for his ability to sleep.

When I was pregnant with Avery, I joked that she would come early. "On June 30, the lease is up," I told people, laughing. "She's being evicted, so she better have her things packed and be ready to go."

I had no idea she was listening.

I rubbed my swollen belly as I thought of my daughter, of how scared I was as I stood in the shower while Chris called the doctor, blood pouring from my womb. Carter was now growing in that same womb; he lived in the same room where his sister had died. I wondered if she left him a note.

I jumped as a string of swift kicks rocked my insides. Carter, who typically slept through the night like his father, was wide awake, bouncing and flipping, ready to play. I smiled as he tickled the inside of my tummy with his tiny fingers. He could tell I was sad; he was letting me know he was okay, that everything would be fine. I rubbed my stomach and sighed, staring into the blackness of the night, thinking of the baby I lost and the one that was going to live because of her.

Avery's birthday came and went. People called to see how I was holding up, and I told them I was honestly okay. July 2 wasn't the day that was hard for me. That day had already passed—the night of June 30, the night I was told my daughter was dead. But Avery's birthday still managed to be melancholy, and I felt I should lighten the mood with candles and a cake. I pictured Chris and I sitting at the dining table, singing "Happy Birthday," Avery's silver urn perched in the high chair, a slice of cake and a flickering candle atop the tray. I smiled at the absurdity of the idea, and we went and got ice cream instead.

Being pregnant helped me through those tough days, because it made it impossible to spend too much time dwelling on the child I'd lost. I needed to take care of my son, the child that had a chance, the one I was convinced was supposed to be here. We all knew damn well that if Avery hadn't died there was no way I would have been pregnant again four months later. I thought of Avery as a martyr; she died so that Carter could live, and I was going to do everything within my power to make sure Carter would live.

July 20 was my last BPP, the last time I would see my son's grainy image on a screen. Everything looked fine except for my amniotic fluid levels, which were getting dangerously low.

"You're being induced tomorrow morning?"the tech asked.

"Yes," I answered.

"Good, because if you weren't, you'd probably be induced today."

I spent a sleepless night tossing and turning, alternating between fear and excitement. With Avery, I was terrified because I didn't know what to expect. This time around it would be easier. It had to be; it simply couldn't get any worse than what I had been through. Yet I couldn't get the image of my dead daughter out of my head, and I was tortured by the memory of the silence. I prayed over and over that I would never have to experience that stillness again.

My alarm went off at 5:30 a.m., but I hadn't slept. Adrenaline pushed me out of bed; the thought of returning to our home with a healthy baby got me out of the house. We were walking through the maternity ward by seven, and I was hooked up to my IV and lounging in bed by eight. This was my second child, my second induction, so everyone, even the doctors and nurses, expected to have a baby by early afternoon.

It had been one year and nineteen days since I had given birth to Avery in a room down the hall. It was surreal being back in that same hospital, bursting with a different child. My room was a little smaller but identical, and I couldn't help having flashbacks to that fateful day. Everything around me—the smells, the sounds, the faces—took me back. It was the same, yet so different. I was so different. I was smarter now, stronger now, and I refused to be controlled by fear. I reminded myself that I wasn't having Avery this time; I was having Carter, and everything was going to be okay. There wasn't any other option.

Noon came and went with no changes, no contractions; the nurse increased my Pitocin. By five p.m. the drip was as high as it could go. I was dilating, but slowly. The contractions were still absent, so the doctor broke my water, hoping to speed things up.

"Things should move quickly after this," the nurse warned. "So be ready."

The more time that passed, the more anxious we became. The waiting was starting to wear on Chris; he nervously paced the room, making me even more uncomfortable.

"Anything?" he asked every five minutes.

My brother called every hour for an update. My mom arrived, unable to wait at my house any longer.

"What can I say, he's lazy," I joked, trying not to panic. I was hooked to a fetal monitor, and the sound of my son's strong heartbeat was the only thing that kept us from going crazy.

Thump-thud. Thump-thud. Thump-thud.

"He sounds pretty comfortable." I smiled. "I don't think he wants to come out."

My doctor, who had been busy throughout most of the day, camped outside my room making a blanket, waiting to deliver my sluggish son.

Finally, as the sun vanished behind the last building, nearly fourteen long hours after our arrival, I started having contractions. They were erratic at first and impossible to time, but before I could wrap my head around what was happening they were constant. I clenched the bedrails, trying to find some relief from the paralyzing full-body cramps assaulting me from every direction.

"Epidural," I moaned. "I'm ready, *now*."

I hoped to avoid an epidural with Carter, simply because I was terrified of damaging my legs again. But I couldn't handle the pain; I needed relief.

The five-minute wait for the anesthesiologist was agonizing. With every contraction came a wave of nausea so strong I feared losing consciousness. I hadn't experienced anything like this with Avery; the epidural had been administered long before any consistent contractions began. Tears fell from my wild eyes as I groaned and squirmed, trying to crawl out of my own aching skin.

A gray-haired man entered the room, and I struggled to sit still on the edge of the bed. I breathed in as the needle hit my back, waiting for the throbbing to cease, waiting to feel something other than pain. Another contraction rocked me, and I bit my bottom lip, tasting blood.

"Almost done," the doctor whispered. "You're doing great."

I closed my eyes and breathed. Seconds were hours. I was trapped in a dark tunnel, running as fast as I could, trying to outrun the pain, but it kept catching me, crushing me, destroying me.

And then it was gone. I opened my eyes and looked around, finally able to focus.

"Did you feel that?" the nurse asked.

"Feel what?" I looked around dumbly, not sure what she was referring to.

"That contraction," she said, pointing to the monitor. The screen showed a large bell curve marking a large contraction. "I guess the epidural's working."

I giggled, drunk on comfort. Avery's epidural was so strong my lower body was a brick. Someone could have chopped me in half and I wouldn't have noticed. This time, however, I had minimal feeling and could even move my legs with great effort. It made me feel better to know I would have some control.

Around one a.m. it was time to push. The room was alive with people, humming with anticipation of new life. I pushed with everything I had, over and over and over again. My head spun from lack of oxygen; a nurse placed a mask on my face so I could stay conscious. I heard a beeping sound, loud and urgent, encompassing the room. I looked around blankly, struggling to focus. A nurse ran to the phone.

"Tell the NICU to be ready, we have…" I couldn't hear the rest of her words.

I stared at Chris, his face distorted with worry. His eyes locked on mine; I could read his panic. He squeezed my hand.

"It's okay, it's okay…" he started. It was unclear if he was talking to me or to himself.

A nurse rushed in with a bag and hung it next to my IV. The doctor touched my arm and spoke. "Since your water was broken for so long, there's not much fluid left to float the baby. He rolled and compressed the cord. His heart rate dropped. We're going to put saline in to get him floating again."

I smiled weakly. "Okay. Okay."

I had no choice but to trust them, to believe that my baby would be born healthy and alive.

Within minutes the room was back to normal. The crisis had been averted, and it was time to resume pushing. I breathed and pushed, breathed and pushed.

My baby still wouldn't come.

The doctor lifted what looked like a Medieval torture device from some secret compartment in the delivery table.

"We're going to try the vacuum," she said. "But I only have three shots with this, so you need to push. Push like you've never pushed before."

I clenched the sides of the bed and pushed with all I had left, sweating, grunting like an animal, one final push that lasted an eternity.

And then it was over.

I felt the release that only a mother knows, the overwhelming mixture of pain and joy and relief topped with a splash of euphoria. I held my breath and waited for the sweet wail, the sound of an angry baby ripped from his formative slumber. I started to panic as five seconds of silence passed…ten…

What was wrong?

Finally a warm, slimy lump landed on my deflated belly. Chris hovered over us, but I couldn't see his face. And then I heard it—small, piercing, angry. It hung in the air as Chris cut the cord, growing stronger and louder as the seconds ticked by. I pushed myself up and stared at the tiny reddish-purple being lying on top of me, squinting at his first glimpse of light, clawing the air with fury.

A nurse swooped in and swaddled my son tightly in a blanket, situated a teeny blue knit hat on his head, and placed him firmly in my arms. I looked in awe at my son; he was so little, so perfect, so alive. His crying diminished as we locked eyes and stared at each other, two strangers who had known each other since the beginning of time.

As I held little Carter Christopher Chandler in my arms I couldn't help but think how much he looked like his sister, how much he felt like her, how much he smelled like her.

I kissed my baby on the forehead and rocked him softly, silently thanking Avery for bringing her little brother into the world.

CHAPTER TWENTY-TWO

There are no manuals for bringing a newborn baby into your life, and there are no manuals for bringing a newborn baby into your life a little over a year after your first baby died. The first few weeks were busy, too busy for me to think. Carter was jaundiced, which required a short hospital stay and countless visits to the doctor. Family and friends were constantly coming and going, eager to meet our little miracle. But once the hubbub subsided and the quiet set in, bringing home Carter also brought back the pain of losing Avery.

At first my sadness didn't make sense to me, and I thought it could be hormonal or maybe even postpartum depression. I finally had my baby, the baby I had longed for every second of the past year. He was healthy, perfect, and completely wonderful.

Yet every time I looked at him all I could think of was his dead sister.

Countless times I found myself staring at Carter's tiny fingers and toes, thinking how they were identical to Avery's. I'd watch him sleep, tossing and turning, his little eyelids fluttering with dreams. I wondered if Avery would have slept that way, if she would've made the same movements and noises, if she would have smelled the same, yawned the same, cried the same. Occasionally I'd catch a glimpse of my sleeping son and gasp, for he looked identical to the picture on our mantel, the picture of Avery taken after her birth. I'd look away, stifle the tears, and push the surging pain back down into its locked room. I consciously reminded myself that they were two different people. I had brought Carter home, not Avery. They might look the same, but they were not the same.

Avery was in an urn on my dresser.

Carter was sleeping in the cradle. Avery's cradle.

The new baby was supposed to be my savior, the child that made everything right again, the one thing that finally completed me. But I still ached inside. The gaping hole had grown substantially smaller over the past year, but it was still there, a vacant space that was supposed to be filled by the birth of my son. I wondered if I would have felt differently if Carter were a girl, if I had been able to dress him in the piles of pink clothing tucked neatly out of sight and supposedly out of mind.

While Carter filled my life with light and love, he did not fill the hole. I was supposed to have closure, but perhaps closure just isn't possible when your world is blown to pieces.

I kept waiting for the hollowness to dissipate, to wake up to "normal," but as time ticked on I realized my missing piece of the puzzle was permanent. That space would not be filled by a son, a daughter, or a thousand sons or daughters. It could only be filled by Avery. The pain of her loss was permanent.

On top of the sadness was guilt. I felt guilty when I looked at the urn on my dresser, as if by loving Carter I was somehow cheating on my dead daughter. Was she jealous of the new baby in the house? Was she sad that I found a way to be happy without her? Was she mad that she had to give up her room for her brother? I couldn't help but wonder.

I felt guilty when I looked at Carter, too, wondering if I didn't love him as much as I should. Would I have loved Avery more? Was I happy with Carter? Would I have been happier with Avery? How was it that having Carter around made me miss Avery all the more? Could he tell that I was thinking these things? Would there ever come a day when I could look at him and not see his dead sister? Would he grow up to be a serial killer because his mother neglected him for an ash-filled urn?

And then there's the question I hope I never have to answer: Would I rather have had Avery or Carter?

My mind was a terrible mixture of confusion and guilt, which made my nights even more sleepless. For the first two months I was a zombie, a walking jumble of exhaustion and shame, smiling and laughing about my beloved son because that was what I was supposed to do.

Yet the more time I spent with Carter, the more I began to have faith that there had to be a method to the madness of life. Babies have a way of capturing hearts, and my little boy stole mine with his sweet disposition and a cocktail of hugs, smiles, and wet, slobbery baby kisses. Instead of resenting him for not being her, I began to love him for simply being him.

For a reason I will never fully comprehend, Carter was chosen to walk this earth, not Avery.

Without Avery's death, Carter would not have lived.

And, while I missed my daughter, I couldn't imagine my life without Carter.

CHAPTER TWENTY-THREE

In September 2009, three months after Carter's birth, Chris was offered a new job 1,200 miles away from family and friends and everyone who knew anything about our lives. While having Carter in our lives brought tremendous joy, a hushed sadness still lingered over our home. It was a difficult, scary, much-debated decision, but we finally decided a change would be good for our relationship, and even better for our family. Perhaps it was our way of running away from the past, but we packed our things and moved from Michigan, the only state we had ever lived in, to Texas.

It was weird and wonderful being completely anonymous in a new place. Moving afforded the opportunity for reinvention, to leave the memories behind and never have to talk about Avery again if that's what we chose. But I found it difficult to make new friends without being honest about her, and, although it often made things terribly awkward and depressing, I refused to make my daughter a skeleton in my closet.

Avery has shaped my life. She is too much of who I am to be ignored.

Through my honesty I've not only grown stronger, but I've grown comfortable with the discomfort, the downward glances, the grasping for something to say. Most people react how I expect, but sometimes I'm pleasantly surprised by those who don't panic when they hear my story, people who actually want to hear what happened and learn about my daughter. Those are the conversations I look forward to.

As Carter has grown my life has become magnificent. My son wasn't a replacement part that magically made everything perfect, but he's brought such unbridled joy to my life that I can't fathom a day without him. I have a house full of laughter and am constantly showered with bear hugs and sticky toddler kisses. We go for long walks, spot airplanes and diggers, go on playdates with our little friends, and have dance parties in the living room with The Fresh Beat Band. Never in my life have I felt so alive.

Still, with every milestone he's hit, I've thought of his sister, if she would've laughed the same and crawled the same and walked the same. I wonder if she would love bananas and Teddy Grahams, or would have that curly mop of thick brown hair, or have those haunting gray eyes that people stop and comment on in the grocery store.

Although she was only here for an instant, Avery has made me a better mother. I don't think I love my children any more than mothers who haven't lost a child, but I do believe I love them differently. I have a patience I didn't have four years ago, the indescribable calm grown only from a journey to hell and back. I understand that motherhood is a privilege, not a right, and I strive to make the most of each day we have together on this earth.

Mingling with the happiness there is always grief, and there is always sadness. Even when I'm smiling, even when I'm completely happy, there is still a small part of me that's crying inside over the loss of my daughter. And I've learned that's okay; it means Avery is still in my heart.

Avery has never spoken to me. She's never appeared as a vapory mist at the end of my bed or sent me any mysterious signs that I'm aware of, although, I must admit, I'd love it if she did. Sometimes in the middle of the night I hear Carter in his room talking his toddler babble, only to burst into uncontrollable giggles. I like to think his big sister is in there with him, keeping him company during the darkest park of night.

Carter and his guardian angel Avery, flying around his room playing hide-and-seek.

As Carter gets older I want him to know of his sister, for her to be a part of his life as she is a part of mine. Even though he's too young to understand what happened, I speak of Avery often, and I hope that she will be someone he grew up with, just another part of our family. I don't want him to think it's weird that his sister "lives" in a container on Mommy and Daddy's dresser. Sometimes he looks at Avery's picture and says, "Big sister," and I can't help but smile.

"Yes," I always say. "That's your big sister Avery. She loves you very much."

I no longer take Avery's picture down when people come into my house.

I am almost at peace with the loss of my daughter, or as close to peace as I'm going to get. But there will always be regrets. When she was alive, growing in my belly, I wish I would have loved her more, hugged her more, sang to her more. Unborn babies can hear the outside world; I hope I talked to her enough that she will never forget the sound of my voice. I wish I had cherished every kick and flip, and I wish I had recorded her heartbeat.

After her birth I wish I would have held her longer and kissed her more. I wish I would have taken more pictures, and I wish clergy had blessed her. I wish I had the presence of mind to ask the nurse to cut a lock of Avery's curly brown hair. I have her ashes, her hand- and footprints captured in ink and clay, and the outfit they dressed her in, but I don't have anything tangible, an actual piece of my daughter that I can touch and feel and smell.

I originally planned on getting pregnant again right after Carter's first birthday, but we procrastinated. As an only child, Chris was happy with just Carter. "Why chance it," he said. I often thought he was right, but I couldn't rob my son of the opportunity to have a living sibling. But I started running regularly and entering races, and it felt good to get back to my regular, pre-baby self. I was having too much fun not being pregnant, and as the months went by, I kept putting it off.

I was also scared. Not so much because I worried something would go wrong, but because I knew it was going to be my last pregnancy.

I was afraid I might not ever get my girl.

As much as I loved having a son, I still needed that daughter. For a year I religiously charted my menstrual cycle to calculate my ovulation schedule. I researched various conception methods that made a girl more probable. I bought into the folk wisdom and ate fish and green leafy vegetables every day.

Six weeks shy of my thirty-fifth birthday we started trying.

I immediately got pregnant.

Unlike the other two, my third child awarded me with wretched morning sickness. For seven weeks I survived on a diet of pizza and Egg McMuffins. Dragging myself out of bed in the morning was a chore. Every inch of my body ached, and the queasiness kept my head spinning.

"I'm getting too old for this," I'd mutter to Carter, the nausea making me a prisoner of the couch.

Every night I'd pray for a healthy baby.

And then I'd pray I'd get to have another girl.

I hadn't quite forgiven God for taking Avery, but I didn't hate Him as much, and we'd been on speaking terms for a while. I couldn't stay completely bitter after being blessed with Carter, but I was still seeking some sort of redemption. I felt having another girl would be the apology I'd been looking for. I could finally forgive Him for stealing my firstborn, and the unbalanced scales of my life would finally be in harmony.

In May 2011, I found out I was having another boy.

CHAPTER TWENTY-FOUR

Even though we might not be ready for it, life moves forward. We can hold onto it, but we can't live in the past. If we live in the past, we will drown in the fluidity of life.

In college I had an English professor who believed all great literature, like life, has only three themes: sex, love, and death. He called them "the three driving forces that make every human being human." As a wide-eyed eighteen-year-old I scribbled down his gospel in case it was on an exam, not fully understanding what he meant. Seventeen years later, I get it.

Sex isn't just for horny teenagers and drunken rendezvous. It's the deepest form of intimacy we can have with another human being, the letting go of inhibitions, exposing ourselves mentally and physically, in the hopes that it leads to something greater, whether it be pleasure, children, or love. Sex can create; sex can destroy. And sex is the start of human life.

Love is the in-between, what we yearn for between conception and death. We all want to be loved. We all need to be loved. And we all need to love someone else. People spend their whole lives searching for it; some of us are lucky enough to be satisfied with the love we give and get from family, friends, pets, lovers. Without love existence is lonely, and we are simply a shell of the greatness we could be.

And Death, the mysterious shadow that comes in the night when we least expect it, bearing his scythe. He will touch us, change us, and eventually take us, leaving a void our loved ones will struggle to fill. Death changes lives, and, if you don't let the grief destroy you, it can also teach you how to live.

It's been almost four years since the birth of my daughter—the death of my daughter—whatever you choose to call it. Memories have faded, yet some remain as vivid as yesterday, like her crimson lips and the earthy smell of her pale, newborn skin. It doesn't get easier with each passing year, but it gets different. The pain dulls and life changes, which makes the sadness a little bit different than it was the year before.

I finally found the courage to get rid of most of Avery's belongings, after months of trying to convince myself that her stuff was just stuff—it was not her. She never used any of it, yet I kept clinging to the idea that by giving her things away I was somehow betraying my daughter, giving up on her and truly acknowledging that she wasn't coming home.

After much deliberation, I donated her effects to a medical clinic for needy children. I found saying goodbye to the material things surprisingly cathartic, like a dark cloud had parted to bathe me in a shimmering ray of light. It was fulfilling to know Avery's belongings were finally going to baby girls who needed them, but I'm still a little sad that I'll never get to use all of that pink. I kept a few things, like the white crocheted dress I longed to see her in, the tiny flowered dress I bought on that March day I discovered I was having a girl, and a monogrammed baby blanket. Those things were just too Avery to let go.

I also kept all of Avery's stuffed animals for my sons, even if they are pink. Some people might scoff at the idea of a little boy carrying a pink cat around the house or cuddling with a giant pink ladybug at night, but I think of them as Avery's gifts to her brothers. And in every hug they get from their furry friends, I like to think they're getting an even bigger hug from their sister.

I sit and watch my son, Carter, four months shy of his third birthday, obsessively playing with his fleet of Matchbox cars, lining them up along the windowsill. He moves them two by two to the ottoman where he pushes them slowly, methodically, back and forth, back and forth. His police car falls over the "cliff."

"Ut-oh," he says, flashing his gap-toothed toddler grin. "Ut-oh, the police car fell off the cliff. We need an ambulance!" He rushes to his car case to search for the appropriate rescue vehicle.

His little brother Preston, almost six months old now, watches adoringly from his play gym, no doubt counting down the months until he's big enough to join in.

I cried again the day I found out we were having another boy, but the tears were brief. Yes, I wanted a girl, but that doesn't mean I'm going to love this child any less. I will always miss the little girl I had but couldn't keep, but I will love my two boys with everything I have. It's very American to want what we can't have, to continually seek out the perfection in life that doesn't exist and spend our time obsessing over the things we can't change.

I choose not to do that. I only have one life to live, and I'm going to live it wanting what I have.

When it comes down to it, I'm actually pretty lucky.

I get to spend my life with my two sons, Carter and Preston, and watch them laugh and play and grow and love, eventually becoming grown men who will make their doting mother proud no matter what path they choose.

And when Death comes knocking on my door, hopefully later rather than sooner, I will not be afraid. I will take his hand and let him lead me toward the unknown, toward the open arms of my sweet daughter.

Avery and I will finally be together again, not just for a few fleeting hours of sadness and tears, but for eternity.

ACKNOWLEDGMENTS

Thanks to my parents, for always encouraging me to take the road less traveled; to my husband, for helping me realize that dreams are a good thing; to my boys, for always making me laugh; and to everyone else along the way who believed my story deserves to be told.

ABOUT THE AUTHOR

Heidi Chandler grew up in Gaylord, a small town in Northern Michigan. She graduated from Michigan State University in 1998, spent a few years working in advertising, and eventually settled into a career as a high school journalism teacher. After the unexpected death of her first child in 2008, Heidi re-examined her priorities and left her teaching career to focus on being a mother. This also afforded her the opportunity to revisit her first passion, writing. *Holding Avery* is Ms Chandler's first book.

In her spare time Heidi enjoys reading, running, cooking, watching sports, and being in the great outdoors. She lives in Texas with her husband and their two sons.